# RESEARCH LIKE A LIBRARIAN

## VIKKI J. CARTER
## THE AUTHOR'S LIBRARIAN

SquishPen
Press

# AUTHOR COMMENTS ABOUT RESEARCH LIKE A LIBRARIAN

"'Research Like A Librarian' is a must read before starting your next project. The tools Vikki shares from her years of being a Librarian are invaluable! You'll learn how to properly access all the knowledge that is available today, and not only from the vast resources on the Internet, but right at your local library. Tapping into the mind of a Librarian has opened my eyes to a whole new way of researching, as I had no idea that Librarian's had so much more to offer than just checking out books!" ~Patricia Rae, author of Mark of the Faerie series.

"Informative and very helpful! I pride myself in researching any and everything all the time, but it turns out I haven't been using all of the resources available. So worth a read, and the workbook is very cool!" ~Elle Mitchell, author of I Never Stopped and Sweethearts.

"I enjoy research and thought I was a pretty good researcher. After reading RESEARCH LIKE A LIBRARIAN, I've discovered how much I've been missing. Presented clearly and conversationally, it's packed with strategies and resources to help with almost any research project—from the most basic to one that is highly complex and layered. I can't wait to put all this good information to work for me on my next project." Donna Cameron, multi-award winning non-fiction author of A Year of Living Kindly.

"I love research... sometimes more than writing... and can get lost in it. This book and worksheets are so helpful in keeping on-task, finding verifiable information, and letting us know it's okay to ask questions. A great resource for anyone at the foot of the mountainous task of researching for both nonfiction and fiction writing." ~D.K. Green, author of five series including The Mommy Mysteries series and The Killers Club series.

"Anyone wondering where to start with their research, or wanting to learn how to get the most of the resources available to you should buy this book.

Filled with instructions on how to do things as simple but as groundbreaking as Boolean searching all the way to where to find repositories of information or how to get difficult books via interloan this is a really helpful guide to how to find out pretty much anything." ~ Laura Wolf, multi-published Indie author.

"Learn why saying, "I just Googled it," makes a librarian cringe! In easy, casual prose, the author provides a goldmine of information on how to research well, including links to libraries, museums, and data bases worldwide. She leads the reader/researcher in a step-by-step process, clearly demonstrating how to begin a project, how to authenticate the fruits of the labor, what notes to take along the way, and how to format the final product, all the while avoiding the pitfalls of plagiarism. It is a must-read for any author who takes their craft seriously." ~Short story & mystery author, William J. Cook.

"Vikki has created a unique resource! There's a fine line between not enough research, and wasting time on too much. This book will help you find that correct balance and make sure your research hours are used efficiently.

The book is well structured and easy to read. She clearly knows her stuff and has distilled years of training and experience into one short volume.

As an author, I have to plan my writing schedule for years in advance. I've wanted to write a historical piece for a long time, but have kicked the can down the road because I didn't know where to begin with the research. I've moved that project up in my timeline, thanks to Vikki's book." ~ Wilderness Mystery author, David Barbur.

"As an historical fiction author, research is key to my storylines. "Research Like a Librarian" is packed with research advice, sources for tools, and much, much more. Being a librarian, the author has tapped into her insight, skills, experience, and knowledge to compile this useful, well-organized book. She covers it all! This will be my "research bible" for my future projects. I highly recommend this book for anyone involved with research. You won't find another one like it!" ~historical fiction author Lilly Brock.

"Concise and thoroughly informative. Vikki has compiled relevant, easy-to-follow tips and resources anyone will find useful." ~ Laura Baird, romance author.

# INTRODUCTION

There once was this little girl who had trouble with communicating. She could not pronounce words with the letter "r" properly. Children made fun of her repeatedly in school. She did not talk. She struggled with reading as well. The words on the page just did not click in her mind. But she loved pictures. She could study an illustration in a book and imagine what the words should be saying.

This little girl spent many recesses at school, wrapped in the warmth of a library. She would pore over the pages of books, willing her brain to function normally. She would demand her mind to form the words she saw on the pages. But her little brain wasn't ready, so the words didn't come quickly like they did for all other kids. With plenty of patience, this little girl's mind eventually unlocked the words she would see on the chalkboard and in books. She started to be confident enough to communicate to her peers. Yet, she still enjoyed time in the library. It had become her safe place.

That little girl was me. People are astonished by my story when I share it. I was a kid who struggled with a speech impediment and reading words for many years. I worked hard to learn to read and write despite severe dyslexia. But back then dyslexia was not an ordinary term. I made it through my elementary school days with immense struggle. Many teachers appeared not to realize that the mishmash in my mind was not equivalent to my level of intellect. They dismissed me as careless or willful. I fought my way through my junior high school years, continually cast aside or neglected throughout my time there. I was desperate. I wanted to be seen for who I was, rather than the limitation that could not be named.

I wandered into my high school years with all the traditional issues high school teens' experience. I continued to struggle because my spelling was appalling, and I was a much slower reader than others. Many of my teachers took note, making negative remarks that left me feeling that I could never improve. To this day, I have a recurring nightmare filled with dread as I am called upon to read out loud in class.

If you told me when I was that struggling girl that I was going to have an outstanding career in higher education or

that I would write books, I would have silently giggled.

I am often asked: "Why did you become a librarian?"

It's a dying occupation. Even worse, while in my higher education career, I have had my peers laugh at me dismissively for my career choice. Being underrated was familiar to me. My choice of profession was natural.

I became a librarian because I felt that a career path that included my safe place would be perfect.

In learning how technology could help with my challenges with dyslexia, I began to use it more regularly. As a result, I had grown to love it. I recognized that many libraries were being left behind the digital curve. I saw a place for myself to add value to the library system because of my thirst for technology.

That combined with the personal fight spirit from years of

being misunderstood and underestimated as a child helped me bring my fighting spirit to the librarian world.

As I break into this unique episode of my journey, I again see a need. While dreaming of becoming a novelist, I noticed that my research skills as a librarian were sought out by other authors. Because of this, I have chosen to share my expertise about researching in the digital age.

As I put to paper what I have learned as a librarian, I realized that I am always learning, which has become my superpower! And I am willing to share what knowledge I hold that's specific to the librarian profession. So please, allow me to show you some secrets I learned over the years.

# HOW TO USE THIS BOOK:
## EVEN IF YOU LOVE TO RESEARCH

Throughout the course of this book, I will share with you tips and sources that will support your research skills. Even if you don't seem to struggle with researching, this book can still help you learn new ways to find the information you need faster. Saving you time gives you more time to write.

While most readers may jump straight to chapter eight: "12 Places to Start Your Research Online, Today!" to obtain access to my research sources, it is strongly recommended that you consider a mindset shift towards researching well and to do this, you shouldn't skip ahead.

I am devoted to maintaining the components in this book every couple of years to ensure the information applies to the advances in technology, search engines, and ease of access that come with time, which is the brilliance of the digital age.

One concept that will never change: your local librarian should be the primary source for the latest emerging technological trends. I will consistently invite readers to head to their local library first before sending me questions. I address this deeper as I explain my teaching style in the last section of the book: "The Author's Librarian is In: How Can I Help You?"

As you progress through the book, you will see links to access the worksheets, checklists, and prompt questions directly from my website. Feel free to download these sources for your personal researching needs. I have compiled them in one workbook for you to use while you read. You are also welcome to download the workbook after you have finished reading this book to help you with future research projects.

Use of Work: I have devoted many hours producing the workbook. I use the Creative Commons Selected License for the workbook. If you wish to share part of this book with others on your blog or writers' groups, you are welcome to as long as you make no adaptations, you are not making money on my work, and you attribute the work back to me. If you wish to know more about this licensing, please email me at:

theauthorlibrarian@gmail.com

### Details About the Book Before Moving On

Each chapter finishes with a list of questions to facilitate the research renaissance I encourage. I invite you to utilize those prompts to write down thoughts about your researching experiences, exercises, and examples. You can access each chapter's questions in the workbook for later reflection as well.

You will find blocks titled **Tip** and **Ask a Librarian**. These will be where I share specific tips regarding a topic discussed or provide guidance as to when to seek out a librarian. Here are examples of the **Tip** and **Ask a Librarian** blocks:

**Tip:** Use the questions at the end of each chapter as prompts to develop blog posts for your own blog. If you draft a blog based on the questions in this book, email me at:

theauthorlibrarian@gmail.com

Time permitting, I would love to read your posts. I may even request to add it to my website, giving you a guest appearance.

**Tip:** If you require more guidance in the future, refer to the last section of the book.

Don't forget to visit my YouTube channel where I provide sources and tips on a regular basis. I will highlight specific sources per genre, tips that I did not deal with in this book, and answer as many questions as I can on that channel. The Author's Librarian on YouTube:

https://www.theauthorslibrarian.com/episodes

**Ask a Librarian:** I also wish to mention, I am an American librarian, and as such this book is written with American English spelling. However, I do attempt to provide global sources. As I work on additional offerings and share videos on my YouTube channel, you will find the global sources expanding. If you do not see what you are looking for, ask a librarian.

Download the full PDF version of the workbook for free.

**Workbook:** access your free workbook now before you start reading. The workbook has additional tips and sources. In this print version of the book, I have provided images of the worksheets. However, I encourage you download the PDF version for later use:

Workbook Access can be found at:

https://www.theauthorslibrarian.com/workbook

## Final Note Before You Begin

Even though there is debate in the writing community regarding when one should designate themselves as an "author," for this book, I form no formal designation for the term. I have created this book for those who are working on the craft of writing, regardless of whether you identify as an "author" or not. This book is not limited to those who are writing for publication or writing to make money. This book is for those who write for any sort of project regardless if the writing is for personal, professional, or educational purposes.

This book is for creative individual who desires to learn to use research skills as a catalyst for what really matters: the best written work powered by excellent research skills. In other words, this book is for you.

# WHY RESEARCH?

Building a Case for Excellence in Researching

THE VERY FIRST question we must address is, why research? That question is at the heart of what I get asked so often. It is why I started my YouTube channel; it is why I am creating two online courses for authors. It is what makes my heart dance! I love that question. Before we explore the merits of that question, allow me to disclose that this book will not be the all-inclusive guide to research skills.

Researching well is a discipline. It's an act that needs to be done repeatedly to become second nature. What this book will be is an attempt to answer some of the questions I have been asked over the eighteen years I have been a librarian. It will focus on authors willing to master their research skills.

I believe many authors ask, "Why research?" because they find researching frustrating and time consuming. They wish to get back to the creative part of writing. I also believe that I am asked that question because authors do not know what to use for research, where to find reliable sources online, and more importantly, how to use what they find effectively.

The good news is that researching does not have to be a time consuming, frustrating aspect of the writing craft! The intent for this book is to share the mindset of professional researchers: librarians. The aim is to help you grow in certainty as you are on the path of building your research skills. I tell all my students "you will get out of it what you put into it." What I outline in this book are the tips to make sure that what you put into the discipline of researching will help you get what you desire: more time to write, hopefully using accurate and verifiable information.

## Why Not Research?

I am often surprised when I talk to authors and they tell me they wrote a book with very little researching. I am even more baffled when an author confesses they did not need to do any research at all for their books.

> I ask, "Did you Google anything?"
> Most authors will answer "Yes."
> I will then ask, "Did you visit Wikipedia?"
> The answer again is often, "Yes."
> That is when I follow up with the question, "How did you know what you found was reliable?"

Here is where I hear a variation of the same answer, "Why does that matter?"

Despite my background as a librarian, I understand the struggles for needing quick access to information while writing. An author doesn't want the distraction of researching unless they enjoy the process.

Over the years I have found authors who answer my question with "Why do I need to research?" have one of two issues:

- They dislike spending the time researching, so they do not do it.
- They don't have an aversion to conducting research, they might even enjoy it, but they get overwhelmed and distracted, so they avoid it.

Both of these issues generally result in what I call the "shortcut to researching," or a quick search on Google. We are all human. This shortcut may help to reinforce a mindset that the author is saving time, energy, and even creative sanity. They will justify this shortcut with phrases like "Researching is just too hard."

Research does not have to be hard or time consuming. You can develop the skills you need to be an effective researcher. This skill in turn, will help to build authority, confidence, and authenticity. Because researching is a disciplined skill, it takes a willingness to learn, practice, make mistakes, and master. Let me set the stage with an example regarding why avoiding "the shortcut in researching" is important.

**Example:** Several years back, before I embarked on my journey of authorship, I soaked up every local author book I could get my hands on. One such book I stumbled upon at my favorite local nursery. We were there for my annual plant purchase. When we went to check out, they had at the counter a beautiful book by one of the staff members of the nursery. It was a self-help book about finding courage based on ancient principles associated with the author's Japanese heritage. I was intrigued. I purchased it at the hefty $30 price tag with the justification that I was supporting a local author. I was curious as to the assertions that the author may draw from Japanese culture.

Only about six pages into the first chapter, disappointment hit. The author referred to a quote that did not ring true to me. I questioned if the attribution was given to the correct person. Being the librarian that I am, I could not move on to continue reading. I looked at the footnotes to see where the author found the quote. She only cited Wikipedia. I did not see any additional sources cited. This was when I realized I can share a better way for researching. Truth be told, I still have not picked the book back up to read. It left me with a feeling that the author lacked authority and therefore her words did not inspire me.

I am sure she did not have that idea in mind when she was writing. How many of us write, then research what we need before we hit send to the printer? How many of us just want to get the story out and skip the process of researching all together?

This world is filled with a massive number of literary voices. There are a multitude of authors writing in every genre, plus some writing in genres of their own creation. Your voice has to not only get out of your head, on paper, edited, and in print. You also have to find your audience and sell your work to them. Why would any author wish to waste all the precious time they have sacrificed to get their masterpiece in the hands of readers, only to have readers left with the feeling that the author did not understand what they were writing about?

You may sit here, reading these very lines, saying to yourself, "Well, Vikki, isn't that what my editor is for?" Possibly, if you have a very astute editor. You may be lucky to have a publishing team behind you, with fact checkers. Not all authors will be so fortunate. Many will have to rely upon their own research skills.

More importantly, why would you, as an author, trust a stranger to make sure your facts line up? Your writing is your authentic voice. With my help, you can have the confidence in building these skills to make sure you are not wasting your time or money on fact checking by others, when you can do it yourself.

Will your readers challenge your research? Yes, they will.

How many times have you seen critical voices in group pages on social media, or heard them in face-to-face readings? I do not wish to scare you from writing your masterpiece. On the contrary.

- I wish to help you effortlessly elevate your research skills so you can write your story with authority.
- I wish that if challenges come your way by a reader, you will have confidence in your justification for writing as you did.
- I wish for you to rely on sources that are easily verifiable and accurate.

To help simplify the process of researching beyond searching only on Google or Wikipedia, I will break down the research process into six stages. From there, I will show you how to condense these six stages into three simple steps. And then finally, how to apply these three steps quickly to sources. The six stages of research are drawn from the discipline that librarians refer to as Information Literacy. They are:

- Identifying and recognizing information needs.
- Determining sources of information.
- Citing and searching for more information.
- Analyzing and testing the quality of information.
- Organizing, storing or archiving information.
- Using information in an ethical, efficient and effective way.

**WORKBOOK**: In your workbook, I have created the graphic "Six Stages of Researching" to help you visualize these stages.

## Applying the Stages of Researching to Research Well

In the next chapter: "The Nuts and Bolts of Researching" I will define three simple steps to researching. I will also show you where in those steps you should apply what I call the Three A's of Evaluation (or "The Three A's" for short).

The Three A's of Evaluation are Accuracy, Authority, and Aim.

**Accuracy:**

How accurate is the information that you are using? I have a list of questions in your workbook to help you identify how accurate a resource may be.

**Authority:**

Does the author of the source show authority? Is that authority something you wish to use to strengthen your own voice? Again, to determine authority, you will find a list of questions in your workbook.

**Aim:**

Aim is a focus on the objectivity of the author. Is there a clear aim to the message? If so, is it what you wish to share? Refer to the questions in your workbook to help you identify aim.

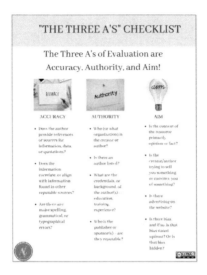

**WORKBOOK**: You can access the "Three A's Checklist" in your workbook. That checklist will have the lists of questions to help you define accuracy, authority, and aim of a source.

## QUESTIONS FROM WHY RESEARCH?

1. Why is research important to authors?
2. How is research important to your readers and audience?
3. Map out your typical research habits.
4. Do you research before writing?
5. Do you write an outline, then conduct research?
6. Do you research during writing with online resource tabs opened?
7. Do you research after you have most of your first draft done to fill in the parts you need?
8. Do you use a combination of these habits?
9. How do each of the above habits affect your writing process? Do any of these habits help your writing? Do you need to try a different habit? Which habit is best for your writing flow?
10. Are there justifiable times you should use one habit over the other? If so, how clear are you with knowing which habit to continue or which habit may need to be changed?
11. How do you demonstrate authority and originality by researching?
12. Why do you research?
13. How resistant to change are you?
14. Do you enjoy learning new skills? If not, what don't you like about it?
15. Do you struggle with knowing what sources are accurate, have authority or what the author's aim is? If so, what steps can you take to identify authority, aim, and accuracy?

# 2

# THE NUTS AND BOLTS OF RESEARCHING WELL

WHEN PREPARING FOR THIS BOOK, I stumbled upon a review of an older book published in 1999 on Amazon for authors on the topic of researching. Honestly, I was amazed that I could not find a more recently published book on the topic. This book had a recent review that was unflattering, but understandable to the modern reader.

The reviewer pointed out that the book was well stocked with practical information, but when the book discussed Netscape and Yahoo, they immediately recognized the book was outdated.

Ouch! I went back to my bookshelf to discover that I had purchased that very book over two years ago. I had hardly opened it myself but did so when writing this book. I have to confess, though I agree, I do believe the reviewer's lack of sympathy toward maintaining reference sources was harsh. Yes, it would have been helpful for the author to have written additions as the digital age advanced. However, they did not. This left a gap in the market. Once I started the process of writing this guide, I was reminded why we librarians are called professionals. There is a lot to communicate regarding researching well. And even more to say about authors avoiding the pitfalls of "researching shortcuts."

That one review helped me to define my goals and reasons. I desire to deliver practical steps for authors regarding how to research well. Likewise, I am committed to making it my business to help others research using the media of books, videos, online courses, and podcasts, and more! Finally, I am committed to staying up to date with the advancement of technology and sources so you, can be up to date too!

## The Foundation of My Approach to Research

- The recognized phases of information literacy, as defined by the discipline of Library Science and Information Technology.
- Years of teaching researching techniques to students in an academic setting.
- My time mastering research skills as a librarian working in school, public, and academic libraries.

The good news is that you will be getting this approach without the belabored years of education earning a Library Science degree!

## Three Steps to Researching Well

**Step One: Define**

The initial step in my process for research is to define what it is that you need. I think of the defining process as posing a question you are attempting to answer. Understanding that you may have an information gap is critical in this stage. Honestly, this first step to researching is the easiest! You will recognize the need to define when you feel stuck. To start the process of step one: define, follow these steps:

- Write questions: When you write questions, you are taking the time to define what your knowledge gap may be. Use the following suggestions to help you with defining your questions:
- Use the 5 W's and 1 H Principle to write your question: Who, What, When, Where, Why, and How.
- Refer to chapter three: "The Secret to Researching Like a Librarian" to narrow down the questions to their simplest research form.
- Don't get caught up in answering the questions. Just get them down on paper or in your computer.
- Set a time for a research session. This research session will be when you go to step two and three: find and evaluate) During that session you will hopefully find sources to answer your questions. I believe that research sessions are the key to taking back your time to write. Therefore, I will go into how to structure a research session later.

## Step Two: Find

The second step in the process is to find the information by locating, accessing, and retrieving sources. This is where most authors will get frustrated because there is so much information in the world. Don't get worried about the volume of information yet. I will cover how to manage the finding and the evaluating steps to help you avoid frustration. Sources can come in forms of books, magazines. texts, online sources, or first-hand accounts.

It is good to think ahead of what forms you would like to

hunt for before you start. I go into more details of those forms in a later chapter to help you decide. Start the second step by following these suggestions:

- Decide what type of source you wish to look for before searching. Which source would you prefer? Will you start on your library website? Will you ask an expert in the field? Will you email a librarian for help? Write that down with your questions.
- Decide where you will start to locate, access, and retrieve your sources.
- Do a retrieval review: how easy is it to access the material you are looking for? Will you need help retrieving the information or will you be able to manage the process by yourself? You may find sources at this stage, but the only purpose at this point, is to see how easy it will be for you to access what you need.

**Ask a Librarian:** If you get stuck in the find stage because you are unable to retrieve a source due to online blocks or subscriptions, make a note to reach out to a librarian. They will more than likely be able to help you access that source or find something similar.

### Step Three: Evaluate

The truth of the matter is, just because you have the information at your fingertips, it does not mean it is excellent information. This is the step where you will use ("The Three A's" p. 7 Checklist) to determine the accuracy, authority, and aim of the source. At first, this step may feel more challenging, but trust me, once you have some practice, you will be able to quickly identify the quality of a source.

The important part here is to know that you will need to copy "The Three A's" Checklist to have at your fingertips when you start to review the sources you have found. Make sure you get that checklist from your workbook.

**Tip:** I encourage you to start journaling about this process as you start to use it. Here are some ideas to get you started:

- Discuss where you have noticed that you have applied "The Three Steps of Researching Well," outside of your research sessions.
- Do you look at social media posts, the national news, and conversations differently? If so, you are becoming an excellent researcher without even trying.
- Can you identify patterns in your researching habits? If so, do some need to change?

## Research Sessions: The Key to Taking Back Your Time to Write

The ultimate trick to researching well is to not allow yourself to become sidetracked down the "rabbit hole of researching!" Hunt for the answer to one question before proceeding on to another question.

This is where I propose employing a timing system to answer your questions. Research sessions will help you stay on track. A time management system ensures you will not settle on one question too long. Coming from experiencing the "rabbit hole of researching" myself, I use research sessions to stay on task. A dedicated research session ensures I make room for writing time.

**Example:** If you have an hour to conduct research on four questions set a timer for fifteen minutes for each question. Use one time block for each question and direct your efforts on that question alone. If you run out of time for one question, that is okay. Finish your notes and establish a date on your calendar to come back to that question.

This is a loosely adapted version of the Pomodoro time management technique. If you do not have a time management system for your writing life, I recommend learning this technique.

**Workbook:** I have created "The Nuts and Bolts Checklist" with access to more information about the Pomodoro time management technique in your workbook.

## Applying The Three Steps to Researching Well: My Favorite Example

After reading about the following example, go to the workbook to apply the new skills for yourself. This is an example of why you should apply "The Three A's"when looking for information.

My husband and I have a shared love for American football, but we support different teams. One season, when my team was heading to the National Super Bowl, my husband messaged me describing all the circumstances "they" knew my team was cheating.

BY THE TIME he got home from work, I had tracked down his source. I calmly sat him down to express to him the many ways that I felt his source was not a reliable source of information. I asked him the following questions:

1. Who was the author of this site?
2. What were the author's biases?
3. How often was this website updated?
4. What did he think the author's intent was for this information?
5. Could we verify these facts anywhere else?

After a few minutes, he accepted defeat. In the end, we had an amusing laugh over my exceptional researching superpower. I am not claiming that my favorite American football team does not cheat, but I wanted to show that he needed to be more concerned about what online source he was using to rationalize information.

**Workbook:** In the workbook, I provide the link to the site for you to practice for under "The Nuts and Bolts Practice."

## QUESTIONS from The Nuts and Bolts of Researching Well

1. Define each step to researching well in your own words.
2. Take "The Three A's Checklist" and write a few sentences about each section. Why should accuracy, authority, and aim be important to you as an author?
3. What are the challenges if one doesn't practice researching well?
4. Can you identify areas outside of your research sessions where "The Three A's" would be important to apply?
5. Identify where you need to grow in these skills and what steps you will take to strengthen for the next research session.
6. Reflect on the example I shared and your own findings from that website.

# THE SECRET TO RESEARCHING LIKE A LIBRARIAN

## The Secret

NOW IS where I start to tell you the real secrets to researching like a librarian. After you have practiced "The Nuts and Bolts of Researching Well," and "The Three A's of Evaluation," it is time to narrow down your research questions to help you find information faster and with more results.

## Keywords: The Librarian's Trick to Researching Well

If there is one thing I love to share with authors, it's how to use the systems already in place to search effectively. The trick of keywords is not new to many authors. They apply keyword searches when investigating new book topics or categorizing their current works for sale on platforms like Amazon.

In the library context, keywords or search terms come from the title, abstract, or text to helps us find the items in a database, on the library shelves, or in a special collection. Librarians will often interchange the words "keywords" with "search terms."

The tricky part about keywords is to know what keywords or search terms apply to your questions. Library systems do not use "natural" language when assigning search terms to a resource. It's not what you would automatically think of when asking your questions. Because of this, many authors will have already discovered searching for materials in a library system can be challenging. However, keywords used as search terms can come in extremely handy once you master them.

How do you identify a set of words to use as keywords?

- First, start with your research questions that you developed from "The Nuts and Bolts of Researching Well."
- Cross out filler words from each question such as "how," "did," or "when."
- Brainstorm antonyms and synonyms that could describe your topic.
- Spell out any abbreviations.
- Avoid abstracts or implied concepts. Some words are unhelpful such as compare, contrast, correlation, relationship, best, worst, pro, con, advantage and disadvantage. We call these words "limitations." I will go over limitations later in the chapter.

**Ask a Librarian:** As you are developing your keywords for searching it is helpful to ask a librarian. We love keywords and search terms. Librarians will often come up with several keywords or search terms that will be faster for results than what you were using.

. . .

## EXAMPLE FOR FINDING Keywords or Search Terms

Original Question:

**"What are the benefits of using an electric car versus a gas car?"**

Why would this be your question? Maybe you are writing a Sci Fi book and the emergence of an electric car is the pivotal point of your story arc? However, to get the feelings of why people may resist electric cars, you can conduct research about what has already been studied regarding the benefits of electric cars.

### Finding Key Words from Your Research Question:

The fundamental ideas are **"electric cars"** and **"gas-powered cars."**

What are some synonyms for **"electric cars?"**

**"Battery-powered vehicles," "hybrid cars," "Tesla,"** or **"electric cars."** Once you have a list of a few synonyms for your topic, you can search them to see what you discover.

**Tip:** Use a Thesaurus if you are having trouble coming up with antonyms or synonyms, you can refer to https://www.thesaurus.com.

**Workbook:** In the workbook you have a checklist titled "Developing Strong Keywords." Use this worksheet to help you define keywords before you start searching.

TIP: Access Online Library Catalogs for help. When you are in your library catalog system, you can view keywords that the library uses for materials, often called "subject" or "subject headings" in online catalogs. If you click on a subject identified in the record of one item, you will populate more items based on that subject or subject heading. Let the catalog and database do the work for you!

## Limits and Limiters

What are limiters when searching for materials? When referring to databases, which most of your research will use, limiters narrow the focus of your search request so that the information received is according to the values you select. Limiters allow you to search based on specific criteria. Most authors do not use this type of searching because it feels overwhelming. Common limiters that will change your results include:

- Full-text
- Image Quick View
- Cover Story

- Journal/magazine
- Peer Reviewed
- Date published
- Number of pages

Limiters can also be more general. Here are examples of what you may see in various forms:

- Limit by content type.
- Limit by subject term.
- Limit by publisher.
- Limit by publication.
- Limit by language.
- Limit by geography.
- Limit by library location.
- Limit by collection.
- Limit by database.

You will more than likely find limiters in the "advanced search" options of the database or library catalog search box. Even though librarians will say using limiters is helpful: we also caution that using too many limiters in one search will bring back fewer results. Limiters can cancel out one another. It's best to try one limiter per search attempt.

**Ask a Librarian:** If you want to use limiters but are nervous about doing so, check in with your local librarian. They will show you which specific limiters will be helpful for your research needs based on the databases and catalog that is used in your library.

**Workbook:** In your workbook there is a "Limiter Checklist" to use when you are searching online or your library databases.

## Google Searching with Keywords

In chapter seven: "How to Use Google and Wikipedia like a Pro," I go over details regarding how to use Google well. Google has an advanced search option that uses limiters, similar to what I described in this chapter. But the rules are different when searching with Google and using limiters. That is why it's challenging to apply traditional researching to Google search.

The first rule of thumb about Google is that you need to try natural language first when searching. Google optimizes natural language for searching where library systems will not.

**Ask a Librarian: To** get a grasp of the natural languages versus subject terms and keywords used in libraries check with your local librarian. Especially if you are wishing to search for subjects outside of English-speaking languages.

### Getting Out of "The Rabbit Hole of Researching"

I cannot stress enough the importance of trying more than one search engine in your research. I will also encourage you to employ the knowledge of your local, or regional librarian. It is important to ask a librarian when searching the library system. This will help you get results rather than spending too much time fumbling around. Librarians will be well-versed in the language used in their databases.

When searching Google, it is easy to feel like it's more efficient. But often it is not the most reliable search engine, and actually wastes your time. I will discuss more about Google searching in chapter seven: "How to Use Google and Wikipedia Like a Pro."

And, I will always encourage you to ask a librarian if you get stuck with your research.

### Boolean Searching with Google and Other Search Engines

If you have never heard of the words "Boolean" searching, then you are not alone. Basically, Boolean is a system of algebraic notations or computer language that helps to refine search results. There are three commonly used Boolean operators that can be extremely useful when you are searching online or in library databases. I cover each of them and provide suggestions how to use them in the following chart. I also cover this in the online course, and we practice using them in our research. When using one of these Boolean operators, place them between your keywords to help make your search more precise and save time. These also apply to Google searching.

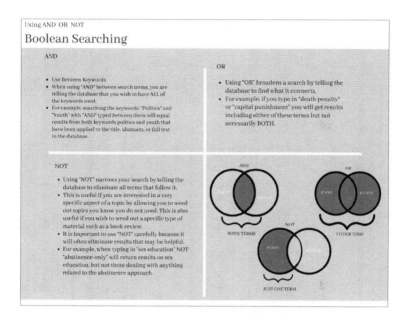

Using AND OR NOT

## Boolean Searching

**AND**

- Use Between Keywords
- When using "AND" between search terms, you are telling the database that you wish to have ALL of the keywords used.
- For example, searching the keywords: "Politics" and "Youth" with "AND" typed between them will equal results from both keywords politics and youth that have been applied to the title, abstracts, or full text in the database.

**OR**

- Using "OR" broadens a search by telling the database to find what it connects.
- For example, if you type in "death penalty" or "capital punishment" you will get results including either of these terms but not necessarily BOTH.

**NOT**

- Using "NOT" narrows your search by telling the database to eliminate all terms that follow it.
- This is useful if you are interested in a very specific aspect of a topic by allowing you to weed out topics you know you do not need. This is also useful if you wish to weed out a specific type of material such as a book review.
- It is important to use "NOT" carefully because it will often eliminate results that may be helpful.
- For example, when typing in "sex education" NOT "abstinence-only" will return results on sex education, but not those dealing with anything related to the abstinence approach.

You can access this full page in your workbook.

The best way to learn how to use Boolean searching is try it out on your own.

Open up Google's search bar to give Boolean searching a try. This exercise will provide an excellent example:

- Type in "kittens" to see how many search results you find. In Google I got about 344,000,000 results.
- Try "kittens" AND "feeding" NOT "4 weeks old" in a new search. From this narrowing of the search terms

using Boolean searching I have only 204,000,000
results.

You can see in this simple example, we narrow down search
results significantly by using Boolean searching. Not that I
would recommend reading 204,000,000 Google search results
for your kitten's care recommendations. I would recommend
calling a veterinarian.

I go over how to use Boolean searching more in my online
course, Research Like a Librarian. We will practice Boolean
searches in library databases.

I am just scratching the surface about Boolean searching. I
cover it in more details in the online course and show you how
to use it well. Boolean searching takes practice. I encourage you
to try it out.

**Workbook:** Don't forget to access your "Boolean Search
Tip" sheet in your workbook. On the tip sheet I provide more
examples.

## An Honest Truth About Researching

Sometimes, despite all your best efforts and the help of a librarian, you may come up empty-handed. That is normal. Unfortu-
nately, that is where many authors will roll their eyes at me and
say something like,

"Researching is a waste of time. I can't find anything."

"Why can't we find anything, I thought you were a
professional?"

I have learned that when these moments arise; it has more to
say about the questions we are asking on the topic, rather than
the lack of materials. It's okay to not find materials. At this
point, I suggest taking a step back to rework your questions

before giving up on your research efforts all together, and then try again!

Here is one example of a question that needs reworking for researching. If you can answer the question without research, then it may not be the right question. For example:

1.) Has the population in the United States increased in the past century?

A better question would be:

2.) What are the factors of population growth in the United States during the last century?

With the first question, a quick search will reveal an answer. The second question will require more searching to answer.

## QUESTIONS from The Secrets to Researching Like A Librarian

1. How are keywords used in library catalog systems or databases different from keywords used in Google searching?
2. How can you use Boolean search phrases to help your research?
3. Can Boolean searching work for general Google searches? Try it out.
4. What are limiters, and how can they be useful in your searching?
5. List places you can go to online to create a search word list.

# ORGANIZATION AND
# NOTE TAKING

## The Trick to Avoiding Tedious Researching

HOW YOU ORGANIZE and take notes from your researching efforts matters as much as where you find the resources. Therefore, in this chapter we will address note taking. Note taking is the important stage that works with step two of "The Three Steps to Researching Well" mentioned in chapter two, "finding" resources.

This is the moment when you record resources in your notes, which will be your key to easily accessing your research.

In many cases, there may be a time gap between finding a resource and evaluating a resource. There could even be a long timeframe between finding and using a resource in your work. That is okay, as long as you have a well-developed note taking system that works for you. If you do not already, or if you tend to use more than one system, I encourage you to take time to develop one system for your note taking.

This is why I address tools that are useful with organizing your research resources. How many times have you discovered something online while you were randomly surfing the web? What if you failed to write it down, and later you couldn't recall how you got to that site?

I used to do that often. That is why I have put a lot of time into thinking about note taking as an author. I am an obsessive web surfer. I have lost too much time on the internet, not taking my own advice of setting aside time for research sessions. More often than not, when I find new materials or ideas, I will forget them. What then? If I don't record the information and my thoughts about that source somewhere, suddenly my spontaneous research efforts are wasted.

This is when researching does become frustrating and time consuming.

After spending months trying different systems, I discovered that note taking software or apps are well worth the time. Whatever the upfront time investment will be to learn, having one system that works is essential. For this guide, I will feature some important online tools for your review. Here is a list of reasons to explain why having a single trusted note taking system is important:

A system will allow you to store your resources quickly no matter when you plan to apply The Three A's.

A good note taking system should have a feature to access offline. This feature will help you to stay focused on your writing.

A system should be where you record citations of resources for easy transfer into your work. I cover citations later on but recording them at the start will help you avoid the writer's rookie mistake of plagiarism.

**Tip:** If you prefer to use paper and pencil for your note taking system, that is perfectly fine. Many authors are successful with notebooks, stickie notes, and binders, or a combination of all of these products. However, the principles outlined in this book about how to avoid the writer's rookie mistake of plagiarism will still apply to your paper system. Make sure you keep an eye on my website. I will be creating a series of notebooks and paper note taking products devoted to those who wish to use a paper system.

## Popular Online Note Taking Tools for Authors

I dive deeper in my mini course, "Take Notes Like a Librarian," demonstrating some of the tools on the list below. If you wish to see suggestions on how to manage research with online tools, make sure to enroll in that course. What a note taking tool boils down to is your preference of format and how you want to access it. Here is a list of familiar note taking programs or apps:

1.) EverNote

Description from the EverNote website: "Capture ideas and find them fast." Work anywhere and capture what matters: your notes - your way!"

**Tip:** Access the link in the workbook for a free month of EverNote Premium using my invitation link!

Access link:

https://evernote.com

. . .

2.) Scrivener

Description: Beyond word processing, you can store documents, images, and notes directly in your writing projects for easy access.

**Tip:** At no extra charge to you access my personal affiliate link in the workbook to purchase Scrivener.

Access link:

https://www.literatureandlatte.com/scrivener/overview

3.) OneNote

Description from the OneNote website: Your digital notebook that helps you organize your thoughts, make them better, and collaborate with others.

Access link:

https://www.microsoft.com/en-us/microsoft-365/onenote/digital-note-taking-app/

4.) Roam Research

Description from Roam Research website: "A note-taking tool for networked thoughts." You can easily access a document and it is as powerful as a graphic database.

Access link:

https://roamresearch.com

5.) Apple Notes:

Description: This is the note taking application for IOS and macOS. It is good for short text and can synch between multiple devices.

Access link:

http://apple.co/37Xr2St

6.) Google Keep:

Description: Included in the free, web-based Google suite.You can easily capture notes and share them with others across the Google Docs suite.

Access link:

https://chrome.google.com/webstore/detail/google-keep-notes-and-lis/hmjkmjkepdijhoojdojkdfohbdgmmhki?hl=en

7.) Notion:

Description: Notion is an application that can be used with all platforms. A high level note taking system that can be used for data management, project management, or knowledge base.

Access link:

https://www.getnotation.com

**WORKBOOK**: Access this "List of Note Taking Tools" you can explore with the links in your workbook and gain access to special offers.

**TIP**: Explore YouTube to learn how to use some of the tools on this list. In my mini course, "Take Notes Like a Librarian," I will go over several of these note taking tools. Better still, I demonstrate how to apply a thorough technique to test those tools for your own needs and purposes. If you do not already have a tested system or would like to consider or learn a new approach, I encourage you to enroll in that course.

Less Well Known But Still Excellent Note Taking Tools

Bublup: https://www.bublup.com

I came across Bublup last year when I was searching for a way to present materials to my adult students who were facing pandemic homeschooling. Bublup is a clever web-based tool that works extremely well with saving websites. This tool allows you to organize websites with a visual approach. If you are like me and you love web design, you will enjoy Bublup.

However, Bublup has limitations. I use Bublup as a tool for creating online reference pages that can be shared.

**Tip:** If you use the link in this workbook to Bublup you will get an extra 1 GB of Bublup storage for free.

TRELLO: https://trello.com

I have moved all of my business planning and some note taking to Trello. I had no idea how powerful and easily accessible this software platform was. I discovered it for meal planning and from there quickly started using it for reconstructing my timeline for my book, podcasts, and video productions. It is easily accessible across multiple devices and there is a free version.

**Tip:** If you need help with how to use Trello, like I did, try watching a few videos on YouTube. I plan to highlight how I use it on my own YouTube channel in the future.

**Tip:** If you use the link from the workbook, you

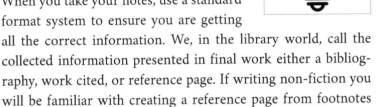

will be invited to start Trello for free.

### What to Record in Your Notes

When you take your notes, use a standard format system to ensure you are getting all the correct information. We, in the library world, call the collected information presented in final work either a bibliography, work cited, or reference page. If writing non-fiction you will be familiar with creating a reference page from footnotes or other notation formats.

There are some differences between each format style for reference pages. I cover only the basics in this chapter. The hope is that you will learn to avoid plagiarism by recording the correct information. I will cover more details about plagiarism later in this chapter. I also explain why I call plagiarism "the writer's rookie mistake."

**Tip:** It is smart to compile some research before you write. Create a reference, bibliography, or work cited page before you write your first sentence. Then add to it as you continue with the writing process.

## Style of Formatting for a Reference, Bibliography, or Work Cited Page

There are several well-known styles of reference pages. It will depend on what you are writing, who your audience may be, or what your editor wishes to use. Make sure before you start your reference page to find out what style you will need to use.

If you are self-published, you can choose what works best for you. The most important detail about a style format is to pick one and stick with it throughout the project to ensure accuracy. Here are the three most common styles of formatting that you will run across:

- APA (American Psychological Association) is used in Education, Psychology, and Science writing.
- MLA (Modern Language Association) style is used in Humanities writing.
- Chicago/Turabian style is most often used in Business, History, and Fine Arts writing (and is the style most editors will ask authors to use.)

By far, your best resource for learning about style of formatting would be Purdue University's Owl Purdue Writing Lab website: https://owl.purdue.edu

**Workbook:** I have created a "Style Format Checklist" that you can access in your workbook. Don't forget to download the full workbook.

## What is a Bibliography, Work Cited, or Reference Page Anyway?

The simplest definition of a bibliography is a list of books or resources referred to in a work. This list should have at the minimum the title and author's or publisher's names. In general, a bibliography should make the list of resources used in the book easy to find by page number on the bibliographic page. Most styles will instruct to alphabetize the list as well. As previously mentioned, the style of your bibliography will depend on the style guide you need to use for publication. Therefore, one author's bibliography may look different than another.

The numbers associated with the reference page may be presented as footnotes or endnotes at the bottom of a page. These numbers may also appear in the text at the end of a sentence.

When bibliographic information is presented at the end of a sentence, it is called an in-text citation. An in-text citation can be more informational. In-text citations often will have the last name of the author included. The exception to this rule is when the authors name is already in the sentence, or when the previous in-text citation already cited uses the author's name. In that case, we just use a page number.

Examples of Footnotes or Endnotes and In Text Citations

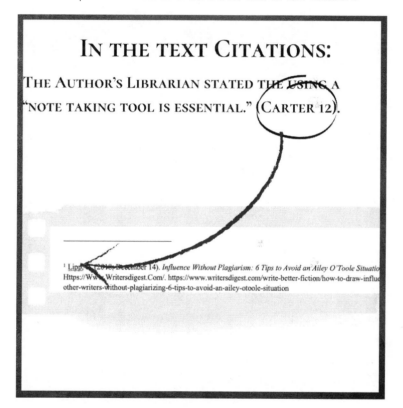

## IN THE TEXT CITATIONS:

THE AUTHOR'S LIBRARIAN STATED THE USING A "NOTE TAKING TOOL IS ESSENTIAL." (CARTER 12).

[1] Lipp, (2018, December 14). *Influence Without Plagiarism: 6 Tips to Avoid an Ailey O'Toole Situatio* Https://Www.Writersdigest.Com/. https://www.writersdigest.com/write-better-fiction/how-to-draw-influ other-writers-without-plagiarizing-6-tips-to-avoid-an-ailey-otoole-situation

# IN THE TEXT:

...iarism is much easier to define & avoid in non-fiction. But authors still need to address fiction and plagiarism. The ce...
...rding plagiarism in fiction work deals with inspiration. There are plenty of bloggers and writers who have shared their...
...ut this topic. However, I wish to refer you to an article from Writer's Digest. Written in late 2018 the article titled Influ...
...hout Plagiarism: 6 Tips to Avoid an Ailey O'Toole Situation is fascinating. 1

**NUMBER OF THE FOOTNOTE**

**AT THE BOTTOM OF THE PAGE:**

1 Lipp, C. (2018, December 14). Influence Without Plagiarism: 6 Tips to Avoid an Ailey O'Toole Situation [Article]. Https://Www.Writersdigest.Com/. https://www.writersdigest.com/write-better-fiction/how-to-draw-influence-from-other-writers-plagiarizing-6-tips-to-avoid-an-ailey-otoole-situation

Here is a comparison of these two citations styles:
In-Text Citations:

- Used in MLA and APA styles.
- Found in the body of the work.
- Used to cite a direct line of text or a paraphrased text.
- Author-date form of citation within the body of the work.
- Placed directly after the quote or paraphrase within the body of work.
- Full citation found in reference page.

Footnotes or End Notes:

- Used in notes and bibliography style of Chicago.
- Found in the body of the work.
- Citation noted by a number, with a brief citation in the footnote.
- Found at the bottom of the page where the work is cited.
- Full citation found in reference page.

Footnotes in eBooks: if you are publishing an eBook, traditionally footnotes are not used because it will be challenging to format for the reader technology. eBooks do not rely upon page numbers; therefore, notation formatting is handled with hyperlinks to the resource page in the back of the book.

 **Ask a Librarian:** If you are stuck on what style to use or how to handle footnotes versus in-text citations, ask a Librarian. They will be able to help you decide which is best. They will also point you to excellent resources for formatting books if you are self-publishing.

*Annotate What You Find! The Key to a Long Memory!*

Authors should make a practice of not just collecting bibliography information but also writing a short summary for each resource. These summaries can be as simple as including a word or two regarding how you wish to use the material in your work. Think of annotating as "journaling." This will be useful when you go back to your notes to use your resources, and is a great way to free up your brain bandwidth to ensure you have more room for creativity.

**Workbook:** The "Bibliography and Work Cited Pages Checklist " can be found in your workbook to help you keep track of this information.

**Tip:** Keep everything you have in your annotated bibliography after your work has been published, even if a resource is not used in the final draft. You never know when that research will be useful in the future.

## QUESTIONS FOR ORGANIZATION **and Note Taking**

1. Do you rely upon memory or do you have a note taking method?
2. Do you have an online note taking method? If not, why?
3. Do you know your style of learning and how it can help you identify the best note taking method for you?
4. Describe one or two tools you wish to try.

# 5

# THE "WRITER'S ROOKIE MISTAKE," AKA PLAGIARISM

IT IS easy to have a discussion about plagiarism with non-fiction authors. Many non-fiction authors will use quotes or other resources to strengthen their work. However, there is some denial regarding plagiarism versus inspiration in the fiction community. Plagiarism is an important topic and could stand alone in a book by itself.

Remembering the idea of this being a quick guide, I am only going to tackle some of the basic points of plagiarism. The key to avoiding this mistake is to be clear about how to handle citations.

## Why I Call Plagiarism "The Writer's Rookie Mistake"

It is my belief, in most cases where I have dealt with plagiarism, the act is one hundred percent unintentional. It is more of a beginner writing mistake. I have found that when plagiarism does happen the offender will honestly say, "I did not know." The good news is that with the correct knowledge authors can make sure that they are doing their best to avoid this mistake. When applying the basics of researching, authors will signal that they are not beginner writers.

## What Exactly is Plagiarism?

In the simplest form plagiarism is presenting another person's work or ideas as your own. Plagiarism is not limited to books or articles. The act can be found in unpublished materials, manuscripts, printed or electronic forms, public speeches, and online videos. People can also plagiarize without realizing it by using other's work from many formats. Ultimately, plagiarism will fall under three areas of concern. This list of areas of concern leaves little wiggle room for interpretation:

- Use of work without permission or consent.
- Use of work with permission or consent but licensing is not documented correctly.
- Incorporating other's work or ideas without full acknowledgment.

## How to Avoid Plagiarism with One Simple Rule

If in doubt, cite the original creator, author and publisher of the work you use.

I feel it is better to over cite your work rather than under cite and run the risk of plagiarism.

## Tools You Can Use to Help Avoid Plagiarism

The good news is that you do not have to create the citations by yourself, unless you really love to do that. It has been my experience that most authors, writers, and students struggle with which information to put in a citation.

There is help. The first programs to explore regarding creating accurate citations will be your word processing program. If you are using Microsoft Word, there is already built-in "reference" tools. While you are writing or formatting you can use the "reference" tab to create your citations in the document and generate a bibliographic page.

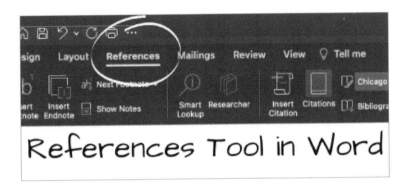

Here is a short YouTube video showing how to use Word's Reference tab:

https://www.youtube.com/watch?v=qr9rtFG7fKM

Mac users will have to approach their citations differently. Mac's Pages integrates with an EndNote plugin to allow you to access any citations you may have created in EndNote. Then you can access them at the time of writing or formatting. Here is the Apple Support page regarding that information:

http://apple.co/2N6F2Cj

If you are using Google Docs, you can insert citations very similarly as you would with Word. Again, here is a very short video on YouTube that will show you how to insert footnotes into a Google Doc:

https://www.youtube.com/watch?v=bD3urjJeVCg

**Citation generation challenges:** It is not about how to add them to the document but rather, what should be added. Out of the three well-known word processing programs, Word is the only one that provides built in tools to ensure that you are gathering the correct information by providing a tool that will prompt you as to what you need to add in the citation. Further, Word has built-in citation styles you can choose from. You will also be able to view your bibliography page as you work.

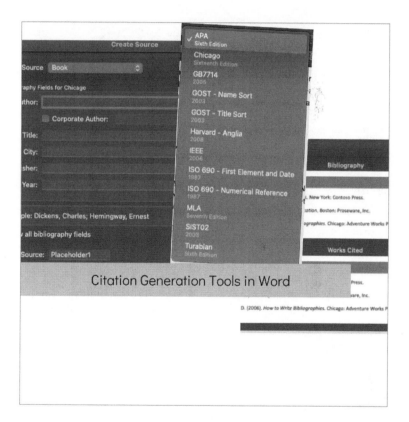

Citation Generation Tools in Word

Here are two online tools that I have found useful when I am not working in Word and when I need to create a quick citation for a source while online to add to my notes.

I do wish to note online citation generators can be problematic. It is important that you understand the features for correct citations first before you use an online generator because some will leave out important information. If you use online citation generators, double check them for accuracy.

**The Citation Machine:**

I started using the Citation Machine ages ago when it was a free online generator. Since then, they have sold to a bigger company, changed the name, and added benefits for a paid version. You do not need a paid version to write a few citations. However, it would be beneficial to create a free account to use if you plan on generating more than two or three citations. I go over some features of this online generator in episode two on the YouTube channel, The Author's Librarian.

https://www.citationmachine.net

**Scribbr:**

If you do not like the ads that can be distracting on The Citation Machine, then give Scribbr a try. I stumbled onto Scribbr as I was trying to find an alternative to The Citation Machine for reviewing on my YouTube channel. Scribbr offers many additional services to help with academic writing.

https://www.scribbr.com/

ASK A LIBRARIAN: If you are working in a library database or online catalog, ask a Librarian how you can generate citations from those resources. Most library online systems, catalogs, and databases have citation generators built into them. This ensures you can generate citations right where you are collecting the information. A Librarian will be able to show you how to quickly export those citations for your use.

**Workbook:** Access the "4 Citation Tools" I highlight in your workbook.

### What Else Do I Need to Know About Plagiarism?

As an author, it is important to have in your writing craft tool belt, the basics of citation writing. However, there are additional ways to signal that you are not a "rookie writer" when it comes to using other people's work or ideas. Here is the breakdown of mature citation skills:

**Cite Your Sources:** as described before, this is the main skill needed to ensure you do not run a risk of plagiarism.

**Direct Quotes:** if you use more than two or three words from another author or source, use quotation marks. Further, cite the source in your appendix, footnotes, endnotes, in text citations, or link to your reference page. This ensures that you signal to the reader that the words in quotations are not your own.

PARAPHRASING: **DO NOT, I REPEAT, DO NOT** merely cut and paste from a source and add it into your work. Instead, practice the art of paraphrasing. Rewrite the ideas in your own voice without changing the meaning. This can be tricky, however, mastering paraphrasing will signal that you are not a rookie writer. The important part is to remember that signal words tell the reader that you are using another person's ideas.

**Signal Words:** Here is an example of using a signal word:

**According** to the author, Vikki J. Carter, (enter your paraphrased sentence here).

**Always remember the rule of thumb:** it's better to over cite rather than under cite. Therefore, even when using signal words use citations in footnotes, endnotes, appendices, in-text citations, or links to your reference page. Here are additional signal word examples you can try:

Regarding what a citation may look like, many authors will most often use Chicago style, therefore, I crafted my examples below in that style with footnotes.

The full name of the author the first time you refer to them:

**Example:** Vikki J. Carter *says* " . . . "11.

The author's last name only in subsequent references:

**Example:** Carter *emphasizes* " . . . "17.

**Here are some signal words phrases with example footnote numbers you can try:**

Historian Edward Gibbons *insists* that " . . ."21

Thomas Smith *suggests* " . . ."4

Lucy Dewlap *points out* " . . ."23

Clark *reports* " . . ."1

**Here are more examples of how to write signal words:**

*According* to Carter . . .

The work of Vikki J. Carter *indicated* that . . .

Carter *asserted* that . . .

The Author's Librarian *acknowledged* that . . .

Vikki J. Carter has **drawn attention** to the fact that . . .

Carter **claimed** that . . .

Vikki *demonstrates* her understanding...

Ms. Carter **contends**....

The book, Research Like A Librarian **supports** authors by...

As the Author's Librarian **pointed out**. . .

As Carter **stated**. . .

Carter **declares**. . .

The Author's Librarian **argues** that . . .

Vikki **believes** that . . .

The work of The Author's Librarian **shows** that . . .

As Vikki **indicates**. . .

As Dr. Carter **implies**. . .

As Vikki Carter **suggests**. . .

Carter **thinks** that . . .

The Author's Librarian **addresses**. . .

How to Use Famous Quotes Like a Pro

Using direct quotes in your work is usually best for non-fiction writing. The general rule of thumb is to quote original sources directly, even if it may be only a few words. Whether the quote is four lines, or forty words, use a block quote in the text. Always cite the individual who said the words.

**Here is what a block quote may look like with citation:**

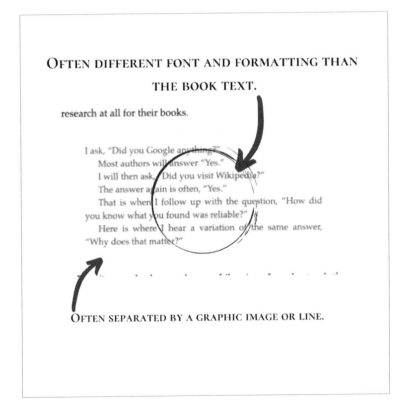

Verify the originality of the attribution of the quote you wish to use in your work. You will be glad you did. In chapter nine: "12 Places to Start Your Researching, Today!" I have listed one reliable quote resource to help you verify famous quotes.

## Pro Writer Tip: Avoid Song Lyrics

Another good rule of thumb is to avoid song lyrics entirely. Song lyrics are troublesome when attempting to use. Strict copyright and licensing govern song lyrics. Here are two examples regarding the use of song lyrics:

- I know one author who wrote her own songs to place in her books due to the sticky nature of song lyric licensing.
- I had to change the introduction and outtake video segments I originally used on my YouTube channel. Even with written permission and licensing permission from the original creator of the song, YouTube would not release the dispute claim that was automatically generated on those videos by a third-party monitoring client. It was easier for me to recreate the introduction and outtake segments using free YouTube licensed music.

## How to Avoid Plagiarism in Fiction

Plagiarism is much easier to define and avoid in non-fiction, however, authors need to address the issue in the digital age. The central theme regarding plagiarism in fiction work deals with inspiration. There are plenty of bloggers and writers who have shared their views about this topic, however, I wish to refer you to an article from Writer's Digest. Written in late 2018, the article titled "Influence Without Plagiarism: 6 Tips to Avoid an Ailey O'Toole Situation" is fascinating.[1]

After the poet Ailey O'Toole's work came under fire for plagiarism, author Cassandra Lipp wrote six tips that every fiction author should remember to ensure they are not stealing another creator's work. I paraphrase these tips from Lipp's article as follows:

- No matter what, do not attempt to use another author's work as your own.
- Ask why you feel compelled to steal work from another author.
- Work conscientiously to separate your work from others. Start with creating a transformative piece based on what inspired you from the work.
- Always attribute original lines and ideas to the original creator.
- Show honor to the creator's original voice by writing a tribute form of work rather than directly stealing.[2]

Here is the article link by Cassandra Lipp if you wish to read the article:

https://www.writersdigest.com/write-better-fiction/how-to-draw-influence-from-other-writers-without-plagiarizing-6-tips-to-avoid-an-ailey-otoole-situation

At the minimum, the most important part of information to save in your notes is a link to where you found the material. This will ensure you will not forget about the location of the resource. You will be able to go back to create a citation when you need it.

Plagiarism Checkers:

With the emergence of online tools for writing there also has been an emergence of plagiarism checkers. Yes, you can use them. However, I find them an unnecessary step if authors follow the basics outlined in this chapter.

**Workbook:** I have created two helpful "The Plagiarism Checklists" which you can access in your workbook. Remember the rule of thumb: if in doubt, cite the work of another person. It is my belief you can never over cite, but you can under cite.

## QUESTIONS for The "Writer's Rookie Mistake" AKA Plagiarism:

1. Define plagiarism in your own words. Have you noticed other author's work that may have been questionable? Why?
2. Write the best method for you to avoid plagiarism.
3. Look at the different formatting styles for citations. Do you know which style you will need to use? Why?
4. How will the information in this chapter help you write more efficiently?

# 6

# LIBRARIES AND
# LIBRARIANS

### Why I Love Libraries and Librarians

BEFORE WE START THIS CHAPTER, I want to clarify that this book, my YouTube channel, and online classes are not to replace the role of a librarian or the library. As I explain in my first YouTube video:

 I want you to get comfortable with a local library and meet librarians, so you can see how beneficial those resources are for you as an author. You might already love your library and your librarian, but if you don't or you don't know how to get access to libraries, I want to share that with you!

I love libraries and librarians. Absolutely nothing, in my mind, can replace them.

## Types of Libraries

It is important to have a basic understanding of the types of libraries that are available. Below I cover a short list of the most common types with access to resources to help you locate a library to start researching. In this book, I will not cover law libraries, government libraries, corporate libraries, or libraries that are managed by private individuals. In the future, I hope to have additional book offerings that will cover more specialized subjects such as genre specific researching and a guide of accessing specialized libraries.

**Academic Libraries:**

Some of the best materials found online from academic libraries are PathFinders (a term we librarians use for Bibliographic Lists.) Here is one example of what these may look like:

**Princeton University Library: List of Local, Regional, and Global Library Catalogs:**

https://library.princeton.edu/local-regional-and-global-library-catalogs

Most of the time, you will need to be a student or faculty member of the institution to get materials from an Academic library. But often on academic library websites they will post free LibGuides or Pathfinders that are amazing starts for researching.

**Tip:** If you wish to access materials from an academic library, but you do not hold the correct credentials, ask your public librarian to help you. They may be able to access the materials from an Inter Library Loan Program. You can learn more about that program later in this chapter.

## PUBLIC LIBRARIES:

I got my start at a public library. Public libraries will be your best choice for most of your research help. To find one near you, or if you wish to access a library around the globe, start here:

**Library Technology Organizations:**
https://librarytechnology.org/libraries/

TIP: Make sure you hit the "More Search Options" to get a narrow search of the type and location right away. Further, under the "Library" tab at the top you can also select a different search such as "Directory of Public Libraries in the United Kingdom."

## MUSEUMS:

Often the most overlooked resources are museums. Though museums are not technically libraries, most will catalog artifacts in a database. These databases can often be accessed similarly to accessing a library database. Many public and state libraries will have access to the larger, well-known, museum databases. A little-known fact: many larger museums hire Librarians for curating collections.

**Start here with the Northern Illinois University Library Museum list:**

https://libguides.niu.edu/museumstudies

LIBRARY LOCATOR HELPFUL RESOURCE:

This amazing database is relatively new, and I can assure that you'll enjoy it as much as I do. The IBIS Worldwide Academic and Library Database. However, it can be a bit overwhelming when you first access it. Refer to the following tips to help you navigate this resource:

https://www.ibisacademic.com

- Suggestions for Searching IBIS World Catalog and Website:
- Download the free IBIS World Wide Academic and Library Digital Catalog. In this interactive catalog you will find a huge list of academic and other libraries listed by subject area. This is an important list to have when you need to try to find a specific topic. Then you can start hunting off of this list for material access in a specific library of choice.
- On the IBIS website, start looking based on the subject area by going to "Search Criteria."

You will want to spend a bit of time reading the first two pages in the PDF to get an understanding on how to use it.

**Additional Links to Global Library Support:**

**APA Global Library List:**

http://www.ala.org/pla/initiatives/legacy

**USA:** https://www.everylibrary.org

**UK:** https://www.artscouncil.org.uk/supporting-libraries

**Ask a Librarian:** If you cannot find a global library from the list in this book, make sure to ask a Librarian. Through their system, they will more than likely have resources to help you locate the global library that is right for you. Furthermore, a librarian may offer suggestions to additional websites to search globally for your research topic.

**Workbook:** Don't forget to access "The Shortlist of Accessing Global Libraries" from your workbook.

## The Role of Librarians to Authors

Librarians embrace the idea that we are the original search engines.

With the emergence of technology, many librarians feared that their roles in society were going to be obsolete. Those librarians who survived developed excellent analytical skills required with the access to mass information. That set of analytical skills, now called Information Literacy, is the cornerstone to modern Library Science discipline.

I started working in libraries right as technology was changing everything! I watched co-workers wrestle with their role because of modernization.

Despite my love for technology, I have always said we could never replace a library. I have gone on record in articles for academic library journals when asked to write about these challenges. I want to make it very clear how I feel about researching in the modern world. We cannot replace a good librarian with general search engines like Google and Wikipedia.

Therefore, once again, I wish to encourage you to use libraries! I hope you befriend a librarian. Make it a habit to use the library as your first stop for research needs. I encourage you to do so, because librarians have been trained in the analytical skills that help navigate the treacherous waters of mass information.

## The Author's Librarian

I always hope that authors will view libraries as I do. If not, I hope to change your mind by the end of this book. Libraries, library online catalogs, library reference materials, library databases, and library staff should be your primary researching resources.

I chose this path because I love to research. I love to help people learn the skills to researching well. Furthermore, every single librarian I have ever met in my career has a very similar serving heart.

So please, test this idea out for yourself. Before going any further, locate your local librarian. Make them a partner in your researching. My guess is that they will be thrilled!

We librarians love to work with authors. My mission as The Author's Librarian is outlined at the end of this book. Simply, that mission is to be the encouraging voice bridging the two communities. I would like authors to experience the wealth of information available at their disposal in libraries.

## The Actions Before You Talk to a Librarian

When thinking about this book for authors, this was the very first chapter I wanted to write. I know the power of a working relationship with a librarian. I want you to know that power as well. So, to make that relationship work well for you, let's talk a bit about how to approach a librarian.

The plan of action I suggest has three things to consider when working with a librarian. We dig deeper into this topic in the master course to ensure your approach with a librarian guarantees a harmonious partnership. But for now, let's walk through three suggestions.

**"I Have A Question."**

Showing that you have already thought about your research questions will go a long way in developing a congruous partnership with a librarian. It is never good to be that patron that leads with, "I need everything you have in here about (insert subject here)."

Honestly, I have had this version of approach so many times. This is what I call the "broad topic" approach. If I am truthful, it is challenging to take that patron seriously about their research. More importantly, I will second guess how much energy I wish to put into helping this patron. Merely because of approach, I will quickly ascertain the level of commitment to the topic. Therefore, I may respond with a similar level of commitment with my own response. Librarians are only human after all!

Because I do not wish for you to be "one of those patrons," I cover how to develop your questions about your research topic in chapter two: "The Nuts and Bolts of Researching." Make sure you take that step before you employ the help of a library staff member.

**"What Do You Already Know About Your Question?"**

To be prepared to help in your own researching, take the second step of the "Three Steps to Researching Well" before you ask a librarian for help.

- Write down what you already know about your topic.
- What resources you already have found on that topic.
- What you do not wish to find.
- What keywords or search terms have you already tried?

**Here is an example:** You need to know what blue whales eat and when they migrate. Let's say you already had some idea what blue whales eat but you were not one-hundred percent sure. You have written your ideas and examples down before you ventured to the library. You wished to have more clarification on the exact type of food blue whales eat.

The notes of what you have already started will go a long way to help the librarian not to repeat your efforts. It will also help them think about search terms or keywords you haven't tried yet, that they could use to find more information with you.

**"Can I Follow Up With You If I Have Further Questions?"**

- Be prepared to ask the librarian how they wish to manage follow up questions. Here are some questions you should consider:
- When is the librarian available for this kind of support, or what are their office hours, if any?
- What format would they prefer for follow up questions? Email? Text? Face-to-face?

Never assume that a librarian will be at the same desk, at the same time of the day, every week, doing the same task every time.

**"Thank You for Your Help. You're a Rockstar!"**

End the discussion with a heartfelt and genuine thank you. Make sure you show support of the library.

- You can always show your support to the librarian by writing a raving review of services.
- You can write an opinion piece in your local paper, sharing your positive experiences with the library services.
- Write a good will post for your blog.
- Make sure you acknowledge the librarian and library by name in the back of your book!
- Further, when the library hosts fundraiser events, make an effort to show your support.

**Workbook:** Access the "Working with a Librarian Action Plan" in your workbook.

### Who Do You Ask?

Walk into a library and you may have to pause to become familiar with the landscape. Often times, it is intimidating to know exactly what desk to start with when asking questions.

There may be clearly marked signs, "The Reference Desk" or "The Circulation Desk." From there, you may see other access points that are manned by staff members. Some of those staff may be smiling at you, ready to help. Others may seem engrossed in a task. Where do you start?

Within the four walls of any library there are several types of Librarians. To make your researching efforts most effective, I want to highlight some attributes of each. There are several possibilities you may encounter. Keep in mind this is a generalization. Each of these roles will have other aspects to their job description not outlined in this book. I added a graphic in your workbook to give you an easy-to-understand basic overview of staff roles in the library.

**WHO TO ASK IN A LIBRARY**

**1 Professional & Reference Staff**

Those in this broad label will hold up to a master's in Library Science. These positions will some of these titles:

- Library Directors or Managers
- Reference Librarians
- Adult Librarians
- Children's & YA Librarians
- Special Collections Librarians

Ask for a Reference Librarian to Help you Start Your Research

Access this full chart in your workbook!

## The Reference Desk

By far, your most important ally in the researching world is an actual Reference Librarian. A Reference Librarian may spend time sitting at an information desk with a title "Reference Desk." Make that your first stop.

Once you find the reference desk, don't be afraid to ask nicely if that staff member is an actual Reference Librarian. Not all of the staff that sit at a "Reference Desk," have the skills of a professional Reference Librarian. Often times, staff are spread thin. Other members of the staff, including non-degree lower-level support, will manage the reference desk while the Reference Librarian is out.

It is important to realize that I am not downgrading non-degree staff. Many can assist with your questions. But you may find it a time saver to work with a Reference Librarian. They have been hired because of their analyzing skills with research information.

If a Reference Librarian is not available, then kindly ask for a librarian who has a specialty in researching your subject area. For example, some librarians will be experts in history while others will be experts in art. However, they may not be required to work at the Reference Desk.

The point of this section is to make sure when you're taking the time to get help, you are getting help from the professional in the subject. It will save you time and energy.

Honestly, most staff will not take offense to you asking about specializations as long as you ask respectfully.

Three Additional Tips to Consider Before Working with a Librarian

- What formats of items do you prefer? Make a note of any formats you do not wish to use. For example, if you do not wish to watch movies on DVD because you no longer have a DVD player in your home, that is a very important fact to know. Or if you need large print books, that is also important to know. Some items may take the librarian longer to locate based on the format you need.
- Is your library card current? Make sure your library card is current before you make inquiries. I hate to say it, but I cannot tell you how many times I have helped someone find the perfect resource in the library only to find out that they were banned from checkouts. Save yourself the embarrassment before you start. Double check that your library card is updated, and you do not have any fines. Most cards can be updated, and fines paid over the phone or online. Do this before you ask for a Librarian to take their time to find you materials.
- Inter Library Loan Programs: One of the secrets about using your local library is the library's ability to request items from other libraries on your behalf. Ask the librarian about their Inter Library Loan program. Often times, librarians will find excellent resource for you that they can request from other libraries using an inter library loan program. Do try to remember that some of these requests can take weeks to fulfill, so while you are waiting, start on another research question. This is also a good time to remember what types of formats you do not wish to

use. If you have a deadline, you may not be able to wait for a particular type of resource.

**Workbook:** These three tips are in your workbook with the "Who to Ask in a Library" image. Do not forget to access the full workbook before you head to the library.

## QUESTIONS FOR LIBRARIES AND LIBRARIANS:

1. Why are libraries important to our society?
2. How are libraries imperative for authors?
3. Do you know where the nearest public library is located? Can you access the information online?
4. Have you met a Reference Librarian? If not, why not? How can you change that?
5. Interview your favorite librarian. Ask them how their services can benefit authors in the digital age. (Turn that interview into a blog post, article, or podcast episode to help share the benefits of librarians for authors.)
6. Write about your childhood library experiences. Were they fond memories or not? How could those memories help shape a positive mindset to support libraries in the present?
7. Explore ways you can support your library and the community it serves. Share that with your followers.
8. Describe a time when you were curious about a library, a special collection, or program. Did you visit the library, attend the program, or review materials in the special collection?
9. From question eight, if yes, reflect on what you learned.
10. From question eight, if no, reflect on what stopped you from moving forward with exploring the library resources, program, or event?

# 7

# SAY WHAT? DECODING THE LIBRARY

### Decoding the Library Like a Librarian

WITH EVERY INDUSTRY there comes a specific insider language and knowledge that sets apart the rookie from the pro. Many librarians will use words that can be confusing to patrons without realizing it. Truth be told, until I worked at a public library, I had no idea how a library operated. I was confused by some of the words I heard when I would visit the library. It took me a few weeks as an employee to decode some of it.

I want to make your experience better than my own.

If you can understand the basics of the function, terms, and services of a library, you will have important keys to maximizing the help from a librarian. In this chapter I will give you a bootcamp version of what I learned on the job.

### The Author's General Glossary to Librarian Language

**Terms for What is Stored in a Library:**
You may notice throughout this book that I interchange the

words: resources, items, materials, and sources. That is because in a library, we will refer to the physical objects that are stored, cataloged, and shared with patrons as one of those words.

Don't be distracted by this interchanging of terminology. You can call it a book or an item, but the function is still the same. It is the material that you have retrieved information from, that you wish to use for your research.

**Inter Library Loans:**

As I mentioned in the previous chapter, inter library loan programs are wonderful.

Due to the extensive reach of online database systems and connectivity most libraries share, many libraries will offer a service under the term, inter library loan. This is where a Librarian or another library staff member will make a request on your behalf, for an item they do not carry.

Because of potential time restraints, try to become familiar with the individual library's policies before you ask about the inter library loans. Most of these policies are listed on library websites under "loan policies."

**Stacks:**

The stacks in a library are the physical shelves that hold the books and printed materials.

**Circulation:**

This term can be confusing for many because the whole library system is tied into the "circulation," of materials. Circulation refers to the process of "checking out" an item.

The entire process of a patron finding, retrieving, checking out, and returning an item is often labeled under the heading of "circulation."

It is safe to say that the act of circulation is the life's blood of a library. As allegories go, think of the circulation of materials in a library similar to the blood that runs through our veins. If that blood stops moving, we run the risk of expiring. Same is true for libraries. If the materials are not circulated to patrons, the library runs the risk of dying.

**Tip:** Refer to the library website for policies that govern the circulation process.

**Holds and Reserve:**

When a patron accesses the online catalog, they can mark an item to pick up at a later time. This is the act of placing a "hold" on that item.

Using the hold system at your library can allow you to make very quick stops to your library to physically pick up a bundle of materials in one stop. Refer to your library's website for instructions regarding how to use the hold features.

There is another possible term for holding items you may encounter in a library. The "reserve" list will hold your place in line to check out an item that is currently out on loan. Once that book is returned, the next person on the "reserve" list will be notified that the item is ready for them to check out for their use. In some cases, a library may have more than one item on a reserved list. Check with your local library website to determine what type of "hold" system they use.

**Online Catalog:**

Long gone are nostalgic wooden cabinet card systems once called card catalogs.

Now, for most libraries big or small, their card catalog systems have moved to a computer system. That system will most likely be referenced as the "Online Catalog."

The benefits for authors regarding this monumental shift of libraries embracing technology is that materials can be searched from anywhere outside the library walls. This gives authors the ability to quickly, without entering the building, create a list of materials before a library visit.

The other benefit of a digital catalog, if an author knows how to use it well, is that it takes away some of the mystery of researching.

**Tips:** Most public libraries allow access to their catalog regardless of whether you hold a library card or not. Academic Library online catalogs can be more challenging to locate on a university website. To find an academic library catalog try finding the library page dedicated to student access. You will find limitations to what you can search, but academic library student pages offer useful researching guides and suggestions.

DATABASES:

At one time in the not so distant past, libraries would keep clippings of actual newspapers. They would store these collections in a searchable system, allowing patrons to access a clip at time. Soon, this rudimentary system was replaced with microfilm and microfiche. Newspaper articles, and images were locked into tiny films that patrons could view through large manual screens. It was almost magical, trust me.

The digital age revolutionized how we locate these types of items. Most have been digitalized and preserved in databases. Library databases have since extended beyond newspaper articles. Here is a short list of what library databases may include:

- electronic index articles (newspapers, journals, magazines)
- eBooks
- images
- videos
- audio files
- conference proceedings
- clinical trials
- reports
- government documents

Libraries will have access to many different databases serving different needs. These databases will go way beyond the clippings of newspaper articles.

It is important to understand that databases are managed by the library's funds. These funds are often generated by local tax dollars or library card yearly fees and dictate who can access the library databases. In most cases, only individuals having a current library card to that particular library will be able to access the items stored on the library's databases. However, if you wish to access an item in a database from a library that you do not have a library card with, you may be able to get that item using your local library's Inter Library Loan program.

**Ask a Librarian:** If you have not used a library database, it can feel a bit overwhelming, but there is help! If you wish to get help with a specific database regarding what it stores, and how to access the information, it is best to set up a time to visit with your local librarian. They will be more than happy to show you the basics. If you find an item you wish to use but your library does not subscribe to that particular database, ask your local librarian if they can help. Most of the time they can request a copy of an article or magazine using the inter library loan programs.

**24/7 Library Services:**

One of the most alluring aspects of the digital age is the merging of time and physical space accessible through a computer. We can now access just about anything, from anywhere, at any time.

But the dilemma for authors is not the actual access of information, but rather what to trust. That is where 24/7 Library Services can come in handy for authors. Due to partnerships, most libraries will offer services accessible whenever an author may wish. Regardless of operational hours of the physical building, you can access a lot through your library with 24/7 services. My public library offers the following services:

- OverDrive: eBook and audio book distribution with a partnership of the state library.
- Hoopla: a digital media service that offers books, audio books, TV programing, and movies.

- Microsoft Imagine Academy Online: computer and technical training.
- Online Databases in eight categories.
- Digital Archive Collection: online accessible archive of newspapers, maps, pamphlet books, yearbooks, and photos of the region's history.

Many larger libraries will offer a "help" feature for an online chat with a Reference Librarian. If you have access to these types of features, I highly encourage you to utilize them.

When I was a student working on my Master of Library Science, I managed reference questions online for the Internet Public Library, which is sadly now closed. I would accept up to fifteen or twenty questions a week. Once I accepted these questions, I would find online resources, compile those findings in an email, and send them to the requester. It was a brilliant, helpful service for students, homeschool parents, and many authors. Your own "help" feature may be similar. Look for these types of services, because they can be a central starting point for your research.

**Tip:** This list of terms and services only scratches the surface of what you can access from a library. The best way to learn about how a library functions, how to work with a librarian for research help, and what services a library will offer you, is to go visit one.

AUTHOR'S GENERAL GLOSSARY TO LIBRARIAN LANGUAGE

**Workbook:** Access the "Author's General Glossary to Librarian Language" in your workbook.

## What Can I Find in a Library?

Now that we discussed some of the general terms you may encounter in a library, let's talk about the formats of materials.

Formats will be the presentation of the information you are seeking. This presentation will be dictated by how or where the item is stored. For example, PDF items are generally stored in a database for easy access, whereas printed books will be stored on the book stacks.

Knowing what format, you may need will help you determine where you may need to start looking in a library.

## BOOKS:

By far, libraries are known for what authors produce: books. That's the easiest one, right? Under books, you may find electronic versions (eBooks), large print, and audiobooks. Again, most authors will be familiar with these formats. Retailers for libraries are the main source of the books collected and stored in libraries.

### Journals:

Academic or scholarly and specific interest journals will be found in libraries. It is most common to find these in a database where you can review a short description of the article before requesting a printed copy. Most printed copies of the article will be delivered in a PDF form. Academic and scholarly journals will be "peer reviewed," giving them more authority, aim, and authenticity. You will not see any advertising in journal articles.

### Magazines:

Magazines differ from journals because their aim is to entertain and inform a general audience versus discussion of scholarly topics. They are written by journalists or other professional writers writing with a goal in mind, but they do not necessarily have to be subject experts. Magazines will be filled with opinion or point of view articles. Further, you will find trade magazines in various topics that appeal to a large audience such as the writing community. Most often, magazines will be available in both print and electronic versions with website access. They also have advertisements; therefore, the clever author should be mindful of the article's aim presented in magazines.

### Newspapers:

Similar to magazines, newspapers provide information for a wide audience, but that audience is often regionally based. Newspapers will cover current events and popular information. You will find plenty of opinion-based articles in newspapers along with advertisements. Newspaper articles will be shorter, sometimes. They are usually found in print and electronic versions, and release on a daily or weekly basis. Many libraries will subscribe to a large newspaper database service so that their patrons can access newspapers around the globe.

**Video and Audio:**

Don't miss out on video and audio recordings that may be stored in a library. Many of these items will provide excellent information for researching. You may find primary historical events in video or audio forms. You may also be able to find actual filmed footage. Secondary sources such as documentaries, educational films, and radio programs can also be useful. Many libraries will have access to a database titled "Films on Demand," that will help you locate these resources.

**Government Documents:**

Information generated by state, local, or national levels of government can be valuable. Many of these resources will include court documents, leadership papers, records, reports, statistics, and international treaties. These sources are authoritative and have a very clear aim. We consider government documents as primary sources. Many documents can be found directly on government websites. However, if you cannot find what you need on a website, many libraries will have access to repositories.

**Grey Literature:**

Materials published by experts outside of traditional commercial or academic distribution channels are called grey literature. These are usually items by organizations, advocacy groups, research labs, governmental bureaus, and independent scholars. Examples can include conference documents, technical reports, clinical trials, lecture notes, blog posts, dissertations, and data sets. Most grey literature will have an informed opinion on a specific topic and will be dealing with the communities in science or medicine. Grey literature will not fall under the popular categories for scholarly work; therefore, it is important to know about it. Even if you do not use grey materials in your research, it is a valuable secondary source of information regarding alternative perspectives.

To learn more about grey literature you can visit Grey Literature Report found on The New York Academy of Medicine website:

https://www.greylit.org/home

## WEBSITES:

Many libraries now categorize and store websites in a database to help authors retrieve information. These databases will help the author analyze websites for aim, authenticity, and authority. Ask your local librarian how they categorize websites for their patrons to help with research.

**Workbook:** Access the check sheet "What Can I Find in a Library" in your workbook.

Types of Collections Librarians Will Refer To in a Library

Where to find items can get confusing because a librarian might refer to the item based on the collection in which it is stored. In most libraries you will find a Reference Collection, General Collection, and more than one Special Collection.

### General Collection

The General Collection will be materials that have a broad range of topics, formats, and usage. To be simple, the general collection will be everything not mentioned in the Reference Collection or Special Collection. Within the General Collection, libraries will break down the materials based on the classification system they use. More about the classifications system later.

### Reference Collection

Reference Collections are books or materials that are high-level overview materials. These materials compile, index, and organize information from other sources to provide a general overview of a topic. These materials usually are not available to be checked out from the library. They are valuable, and have uses by many possible readers, and will be specific in subjects and/or multiple volumes. Most common reference books you can access for researching are

- Almanacs
- Atlas and Maps
- Bibliographies
- Biographical Works
- Resources
- Dictionaries
- Directories
- Encyclopedias

- Handbooks
- Special Collections

## SPECIAL COLLECTIONS

Special Collections are materials designed to fulfill a regional or specific topic. These items are often considered rare. Due to their limited publications status, special collections will have restrictions to access. However, Special Collections are the most often used for researching. Many libraries have started to digitize their special collections, granting access to a wider audience through the internet.

**Workbook:** Get your "Collections Checklist" in your workbook.

## The Overview of How Libraries are Organized: Classification Systems

Now, let's talk about the two systems used to organize libraries. Most libraries within the US will either use the Library of Congress Classification System, abbreviated to LC, or the Dewey Decimal System to organize the materials.

Academic libraries will use the LC systems, whereas most public libraries will rely on the Dewey Decimal System. School libraries will use the Dewey Decimal System as well.

Outside the US, it is reported that over 135 libraries use the Dewey Decimal System.

To access a regional list of world libraries that use the Dewey Decimal System, you can visit this link:

https://www.oclc.org/en/dewey/resources/countries.html

DON'T GET TOO worried when thinking about the classification systems. Librarians love the classification system they use. We do not expect those we serve to love it, understand it, or even see it. That is why we are here, so don't be afraid to ask a librarian or staff member for help.

In my online course I will share some secrets about how to use the LC or the Dewey Decimal System for advanced scanning on library stacks.

**Workbook:** Access my "Library Classification Checklist" in your workbook.

The Best Resources to Start Researching: Pathfinders or LibGuides

These lists are curated resource lists created by librarians. These lists can be varied on topics and are extremely useful when starting your research.

You can find many of these lists published online through library websites. I love pathfinders also known as library guides. What makes pathfinders valuable is that the librarians narrow down the topic for you. They will highlight reliable sources to explore, cutting out much of the work. Plus, most of these types of lists will have a large range of resources listed. This provides variety of access. If you are using a pathfinder not from your local library, don't forget to ask your librarian how they can help you gain access to some of the sources on the pathfinder.

**Workbook:** I have a list of excellent pathfinders to help get your research started from my own personal list. You can access the "List of Pathfinders & Library Guides" in your workbook.

## QUESTIONS TO SAY WHAT? **Decoding the Library**

1. Reflect on a moment in time when you had to learn a new skill. Did that skill come with its own set of terms to navigate? If so, how did you do?

2. Are there library terms you knew already? Are there some you did not know? How is having an idea of library terms helpful when you are speaking to a Librarian?

3. What is the hardest part for you regarding access to online catalogs? Can you identify three steps to try to help you move past that obstacle?

4. Have you ever accessed a pathfinder or LibGuide? If so, reflect on how that guide helped you in your research. What would you have added? What would you have deleted from the guide?

5. If not, write down one subject on which you wish to find a pathfinder or LibGuide. Can you find one from searching online library websites? If not, have you asked your local Librarian about the topic? Reflect on that experience. Was it helpful in your researching? Did you gain more resources? If not, what could you have done differently to gain the information you needed?

6. What formats of resources do you prefer, and why? Have there been times you wanted a specific format but needed to use what was available? If yes, how did that go for you? If not, would you consider using a resource regardless of the format and how would you go about using that presentation?

# 8

# HOW TO USE GOOGLE AND WIKIPEDIA LIKE A PRO

How to Use Google & Wikipedia

INTERNET SEARCHING (and researching) has quickly become the fastest way to locate and consume information. But don't take my word for it, consider the Pew Research Center. In two articles published on their website in 2010, they outlined how often each generation would use the internet for information and the patterns of reliance Americans face with researching information online before making important decisions. According to these articles, "seventy-nine percent of all Americans go online" for their searching needs.[1]

I would not be surprised if that number has increased since 2010.

The overwhelming fact is that across the board, the popularity of deliberately using the internet for searching spans across all generations from Millennials to the Silent Generation, according to another Pew Research article published in 2010.[2]

Read these two fascinating reports from the Pew Research Center:

Most Americans Rely on Their Own Research to Make Big Decisions, and That Often Means Online Searches:

https://www.pewresearch.org/fact-tank/2020/03/05/most-americans-rely-on-their-own-research-to-make-big-decisions-and-that-often-means-online-searches/

Generations Online 2020:

https://www.pewresearch.org/internet/2010/12/16/generations-2010/

The articles from Pew Research Center didn't surprise me. It is what we librarians had already guessed.

Many will rely on their own research, often using unreliable commonly used search engines such as Google or Wikipedia before making decisions. This also identifies a trend in how people conduct research for writing in the modern age.

In an informal poll I use before making an appearance to writer's groups to discuss researching habits, I asked the following question of the participants:

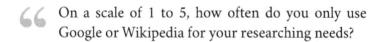

On a scale of 1 to 5, how often do you only use Google or Wikipedia for your researching needs?

I asked participants to identify where they conduct their research. Labeling the number one: "Never, ever would I use Google or Wikipedia for my researching needs." To number five: "I only use Google or Wikipedia for my researching needs."

The results of my questions were:

- 66.7% of those who participated answered level three. This indicates these participants would research with Google or Wikipedia often.
- 33% were in level four for this survey question, indicating they were heavily using Google and Wikipedia for their researching needs.

If you are in the habit of going to these search engines first, I have a suggestion for you: go beyond Google and Wikipedia! Find a reliable starting point for your research like library guides or pathfinders. Access Google and Wikipedia for other reasons, if you must.

If you only use Google or Wikipedia for your research, I have an even stronger suggestion: **Stop!** Expand your researching method to using reliable resources suggested in this book.

I will now provide a few recommendations for using both of these search engines well, if you really must:

### Let the Experts Do the Dirty Work

Google and Wikipedia are well known in the library and academic community as being useful for idea generation. However, they are not respected for use as the main source of researching. If you look back to the discussion in chapter two regarding aim, authority, and authenticity, you should be able to understand why the library and academic community frowns on researching only by means of Google and Wikipedia.

Sure, these search engines are quick and always available. They may even feel legitimate, but how do you know?

Your research can be very problematic when attempting to "prove" your research when you only rely upon one search engine. Why would you rely upon a search engine that has been recognized already as being questionable regarding authority, accuracy, objectivity, currency, and amount of perspective in coverage?

Whereas curated databases and resources provided by a library have gone through a strict proofing method for their resources.

Why take a risk on your own, when you can have the experts

do the work for you?

Google and Wikipedia are perfectly okay to "start searching" a concept. They are useful to help narrow down your researching needs. But do not stay there. I will repeat, because it is worth saying it again, go beyond Google and Wikipedia!

## Google: Suggestions for Use When Researching

**Spelling, definitions, word choice, and "hearing" a word:**

My favorite way to use Google stems from my disorder. Since I have dyslexia, I struggle with word choice in written form. I also struggle with the spellings of words that are extremely similar to one another. I do not see the mistakes on paper. I have to hear them before I know there is a mistake. Often, I am confused by the spelling of words unless I can hear the mistake. Dyslexia is a disorder of interpretation of words, letters, numbers, or symbols. This disorder does not affect the intellect of the individual, it only makes the tasks of writing or reading more challenging.

Because of this, I learned to use Google when I am editing. Usually starting with my first self-edit, I will rely on Google for quick word meaning, spelling, and definitions.

Because I have to read my work out loud during the editing process, I have become accustomed to identifying a word using Google's speech to text feature in the dictionary.

**Word Origin and Meaning:**

The origin feature in Google's dictionary is very important when writing historical fiction (and other genres) to avoid slang terms. One example is the word "great."

I used the word "great" in a sentence similar to this one: "I know you are not feeling great." However, the word "great" was not used in the time period in which my writing was taking place. As a result, I changed the word to "well."

Another example is how I use Google to help me with the meanings of words. I was scheduled to write an endorsement for a book I was reading. While reading this book, I stumbled upon a word I could not decipher from the text. I honestly had no idea what the word "confab" meant.

Doing a quick Google search helped me to see that "confab" was a noun labeling "an informal private conversation or discussion." This information was generated from Google's English dictionary provided by Oxford Languages.[3]

After finding this meaning, I quickly moved on with reading the story.

There are many more useful reasons to use Google when researching including accessing Google Books and Google Scholar. I cover those benefits in my online course Research Like a Librarian, as well as highlight them on my YouTube channel.

## Beware of Wikipedia

The hit pop culture American version of "The Office" shares my favorite quote about Wikipedia. In one of the episodes the character Michael Scott explained, in all seriousness, why he loved Wikipedia:

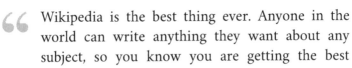 Wikipedia is the best thing ever. Anyone in the world can write anything they want about any subject, so you know you are getting the best possible information.[4]

### The Function of Wikipedia:

Putting aside the humor of Michael Scott's belief of the accuracy of the information on Wikipedia, authors need to dive deeper into why this comedic quote is so important. First, it is important to understand the functionality of Wikipedia. This functionality is why I, and every other Librarian across the globe will exercise strong caution when using Wikipedia for research. It is also why you will see Librarians physically cringe when an author tells us Wikipedia is the only place they conduct research.

As Wikipedia states on their "about" page, "Wikipedia is an online free-content encyclopedia project helping to create a world in which everyone can share in the sum of all knowledge." [5]

Truthfully, I love the principle behind Wikipedia, however, from a Librarian's standpoint, here is where my researching mindset, and eventually yours I hope, will see the problem with verifying information on Wikipedia. Their website goes on to state that their content is based on "freely editable content." Further, "Wikipedia is written collaboratively by largely anonymous volunteers who write without pay." [6]

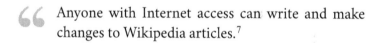 Anyone with Internet access can write and make changes to Wikipedia articles. [7]

These anonymous volunteers are expected to follow the fundamental principles, policies, and guidelines that have been created by the Wikipedia community. To be fair, Wikipedia clearly provides a disclaimer, but I fear many authors and readers may miss this disclaimer. Once you read it, it can be alarming when thinking that these pages are open for additions and edits by anyone.

The principle behind Wikipedia is powerful, however with over 900 million edits, 1,115 administrators, over 40 million registered users, and over 6 million articles loosely monitored by anonymous volunteers, at the time of writing this book, the

Librarian in me cannot help but take note about all the concerns regarding accuracy.[8]

DO NOT USE WIKIPEDIA FOR YOUR ONLY RESOURCE! PERIOD!

I am not alone with my concerns. This quote from one of my favorite international indie authors, Joanna Penn, in her book, How to Write Non-Fiction, discusses the need to explore beyond Wikipedia:

> Go beyond Wikipedia to verify dates, quotes, studies, scientific papers, and publications. [9]

Penn continues in her book to explain how she uses peer reviewed resources for her work. She also shares how that information is clearly identified in her indexes at the end of her books.

Academic Libraries across the globe share the same messaging for their students when instructing research:

DON'T CITE WIKIPEDIA AS A SOURCE. EVER!

**How to Use Wikipedia like a Pro:**

It is okay to use Wikipedia as your starting point for research as long as you remember to apply The Three A's: accuracy, authority, and aim.

Use Wikipedia when you wish to discover search terms, key words, or general topics. Make sure you look at the bottom of the Wikipedia page to discover sources. That is one of the best aspects of Wikipedia. But remember these steps if using Wikipedia as a starting point:

---

### Example of a Wikipedia Source List at the Bottom of a Wikipedia Page:

19. ^ Former Blues goalkeeper Peter Goy has died aged 82 ⟨⟩
20. ^ Angèle Jacq, autrice et défenseuse de la langue bretonne, est décédé
21. ^ Former BJP MLA Pascal Dhanare dead ⟨⟩
22. ^ Актриса из "Бриллиантовой руки" Серафима Холина найдена ме| Russian)
23. ^ Advokat Tor Kjærvik (70) drept på Røa ⟨⟩ (in Norwegian)
24. ^ На Рівненщині померла відома діячка культури ⟨⟩ (in Ukrainian)
25. ^ Mort de l'écrivain d'origine autochtone Michel Noël à 76 ans ⟨⟩ (in Fren
26. ^ Luto en el periodismo antioqueño por la muerte de Rodrigo Pareja ⟨⟩ (i
27. ^ John Pelan (1957-2021) ⟨⟩
28. ^ अवसान:इतिहासकार पद्मश्री डॉक्टर योगेश प्रवीण का निधन⟨⟩ (in Hindi)

---

- Do not make Wikipedia your primary source.
- Always check reliability of the sources in the articles you read on Wikipedia with other reliable sources.

**Tip:** In my online course, I will show you my favorite way to use Wikipedia regarding how to define search terms and keywords.

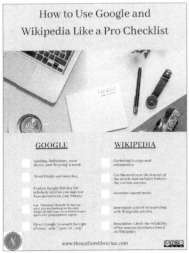

**Workbook:** I created "How to Use Google and Wikipedia Like a Pro Checklist," found in your workbook.

**QUESTIONS for How to Use Google and Wikipedia Like a Pro**

1. Reflect on my observations about Google and Wikipedia regarding their roles in researching. Do you agree? If not, why? If so, how can you expand your view of researching?
2. What does the future hold for researching regarding Google and Wikipedia? Interview people you know a few generations below you. Ask them what their views of Google and Wikipedia are for research. Explore those reactions and how you feel about what they have to say.

# 9

# 12 PLACES TO START YOUR RESEARCH ONLINE, TODAY!

I HAD A VERY hard time narrowing down just twelve for you. I also struggled with defining exactly how to recommend across genres. I have hundreds of sources for almost every genre on my own personal research lists, which I plan to talk about on my YouTube channel. Make sure you check there often.

I have heard from many authors that they need a place to start. That is the essence of this chapter, a starting point for authors, but this is by no means the ending. I encourage you to use the tools and information provided in this book to expand your own personal research list. Because there's a vast number of excellent sources I could not just provide twelve. Therefore, I also share two bonus ideas for enhancing your research! Some suggestions on this list will be Library Guides (aka LibGuides,) or Pathfinders: I discuss the usefulness of library guides and pathfinders in chapter six. These lists are excellent resources to start your researching. Bookmark them when you find them.

**Genealogical Research:** You may notice the absence of sources in this book and my discussion online about genealogical research. This is due to the fact that genealogical research, though very exciting, is out of my scope of expertise. I encourage authors, when they ask about genealogical records to start with their local genealogical societies. These societies are often associated with local libraries.

You can also start your genealogical research for US sources by going to the National Archives by The U.S. National Archives and Records Administration:

https://www.archives.gov/research/alic/
reference/genealogy.html

For UK genealogical research, you can start with The National Archives Research Guide by UK Government Web Access:

https://www.nationalarchives.gov.uk/help-with-your-research/research-guides/medieval-early-modern-family-history/

Difference Between Primary Sources and Secondary Sources

Before you dive into the twelve sources I have compiled for you, I wish to take a moment to discuss the difference between primary sources and secondary sources. I would encourage authors, when they can, to attempt to use as many primary sources as possible. The reference to primary sources and secondary sources was touched upon in chapter six, but I wanted to devote a section to their exact definitions.

**Primary Sources are Original Documents:**

When possible, use a primary source for your researching needs. As an author, you will find a wealth of ideas that can be generated from these original sources. Original sources include:

- Diaries
- Speeches
- Manuscripts
- Letters
- Interviews
- Records
- Eyewitness Accounts (mentioned in Chapter ten: "Finding Your Secret Agent")
- Autobiographies
- Empirical scholarly works (research articles, clinical reports, case studies, dissertations)
- Creative works (poetry, music, video, photography)

**Secondary Sources:**

Secondary sources are still very useful; however, authors should remember that they draw from original documents. If you can get access to those original documents, you will show you understand accuracy, authority, and aim. Secondary sources will describe, summarize, discuss, or provide details from original sources. Frankly, the author of a secondary resource did not participate in the events they discuss, however, they may have used an original source to help shape the details, summaries, or events mentioned. These sources can include:

- Textbooks
- Magazine Articles
- Book Reviews
- Commentaries
- Encyclopedias
- Almanacs

Secondary sources are perfect when you are still developing your questions to research. By referring to secondary sources, you will be able to identify the keywords or search terms needed to find more information. Further, when reviewing secondary sources, you will be directed to the primary source discussed, making your research time more efficient.

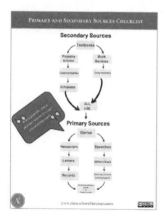

**Workbook:** Access the "Primary and Secondary Sources Checklist" in your workbook.

## WorldCat: The Librarian's Go To for Research

The number one tool that I wish to share with you is one you may not have heard about. It has long been a librarian's source for locating materials worldwide, however, this tool is not limited to librarians use. It is the OCLC WorldCat online catalog. The WorldCat is short for World Catalog system and is managed by the WorldCat organization. The WorldCat is the world's largest network of library catalogs. It is excellent for being the first point of access for searching resources on the web.

**Find WorldCat here:**

https://www.worldcat.org

I AM ONLY INTRODUCING the idea of it to you here in this book. To learn more about this tool and the many excellent applications for researching, I recommend joining me in my master course, "Research Like A Librarian." In that online course, I will demonstrate how to develop your research questions from start to finish. We will start our research with the WorldCat tools.

## The List of 12 Places to Start Your Research, Today!

## Maps of US: The Library of Congress Digital Collection > Maps

If you do not already know about the Library of Congress Digital Collections, then you may have been missing out on one of the best online research tools available.

Visit the link to their special collections of maps. But honestly, don't stop with just the map collection. You can explore so much more from this website. I highly recommend you bookmark and explore the Library of Congress Digital Collection often.

Access website:

https://www.loc.gov/collections/?fa=original-format:map

## Historic England

If the UK is where you are needing resources, I suggest starting with the Historic England website. This website's primary collection houses listings in England dating pretty far back in history. They have advice on the website regarding how to conduct research including access to a collection of books and images that could spark your interest. Looking at dwelling spaces from the past can be an important part of your research for settings, places, and times.

Access website: https://historicengland.org.uk/

## SHAFR Task Force

Don't be side-tracked by the title, this list is excellent. It is created by The Society for Historians of American Foreign Relations. This bibliography of electronic resources listed by nation or region. This list is a very good starting point for global researching. Be sure to go to the "Aggregators by Subject" if you are overwhelmed with the mass volume of this site.

Access website:

https://shafr.org/research/archives-resources/digital

## World Newspaper Researching

I am asked most often how to access world newspapers, which is a brilliant question. I have found that authors who need newspapers from their area, have discovered archives from their local or state libraries. However, world newspapers can feel more challenging when it comes to researching. My tried and true first resource I recommend is Elephind. This powerful search engine will allow you to search across their collection of over 3,000,000 worldwide newspapers. They provide a page on search tips, getting started, and a content updates schedule. They even allow you to create a free account to keep your search results organized with bookmarks and comments.

Access website: https://www.elephind.com

## World History Primary SOURCES

If you need to dig deeper into world history, then I highly recommend this World History source. This resource is brilliantly designed with clearly defined help sections such as "Finding World History." You can review scholarly online primary sources in the "Unpacking Evidence" section. Plus, you can access eight guides written by world leading historical scholars teaching you how to analyze primary resources. The "Analyzing Documents" section is eight multimedia case studies highlighting strategies for interpreting media sources. They also offer an online world history survey course.

If you already know what you need to look for, start with the "Finding World History" section.

Access website:
https://chnm.gmu.edu/worldhistorysources/index.html

## World Digital Library Master List by McMaster University

Exploring world digital library collections is the great way to start your researching. Now more than ever, digital libraries are becoming more accessible. Here is an excellent master list of digital collections by themes. This list is compiled by the McMaster University Libraries. The aim is to help you get started with searching digital library collections.

Access website:

https://medhumanities.mcmaster.ca/index/libraries-archives-museums/digital-collections/digital-collections--master-list

## Eyewitness to History

Nothing can beat learning about history from the eyes of those who lived it. This website is an excellent place to start your research with primary resources. I enjoy the photo of the week! This collection spans ancient world history to the 20th century:

Access website:

http://www.eyewitnesstohistory.com/eyindx.htm

## THE BRITISH LIBRARY Catalogue and Collections

This collection is one that I visit often when I am conducting research for my historical fiction novel. They provide access to books, journals, manuscripts, maps, stamps, music, patents, photographs, and newspapers. Many of these items are freely accessible online.

Access website:

https://www.bl.uk/catalogues-and-collections

## The World Digital Library

An excellent resource for locating primary source materials is by searching the collection of over 19,000 items found on the

World Digital Library. This collection spans from 193 countries, with a historical scope starting around 8000 BCE and expands to the early 21st century. What I appreciate about this digital library collection is that you can change the language before you start searching. The collection can be searched in seven languages.

If you need help searching this site, locate at the top of the main page a tab that says "explore." This tab will allow you to explore by historical themes. These themes are broken down by place, time period, topic, type of item, language, and institution.

Access website: https://www.wdl.org

## Library Spot

Aesthetics aside, when it comes to the sheer volume of resources listed, this may become your "go to" page to start your researching. Not only do they have a large online list of links, but they are also managed in logical order. The one thing to be mindful about regarding this site, is that they have advertisements on the pages. If you can ignore the advertisements, the volume of links in the Reference Desk section alone are highly valuable. It should be noted that Library Spot tends to focus on the US.

Access website: http://www.libraryspot.com

## Online Museum Resources List By Museum Computer Network

Museums now offer many of their collections, artifacts, and documents for viewing online. With the hit of the 2020 global pandemic, more and more museums developed virtual access to their resources. I often find when speaking with authors, many forget about world museums. With the advancement of technology, authors do not necessarily need to leave their own homes to gather relevant resources from museums. This list is provided by the MCN organization. This organization assists museums with technology:

Access website:

https://mcn.edu/a-guide-to-virtual-museum-resources/

**WORKBOOK**: Access the abbreviated version of the "12 Places to Start Your Research, Today," in your workbook. This list only includes the links.

## BONUS # 1: Lit Quotes

If you wish to verify a quote go to this website, which is dedicated to that very function.

Access website: https://www.litquotes.com

## BONUS #2: The Gutenberg Project

As a Librarian student I worked on the Gutenberg Project. This site has grown considerably since those days. It's a good place to look for eBooks for your research needs. The good news is that in 2020 they have updated their website to be more user-friendly. This is an improvement from the site that I worked with as a student. Start your search by going to "Search and Browse" tab at the top of left of the page, and then select the "Bookshelf" tab:

Access website: http://www.gutenberg.org

**WORKBOOK**: You can find The "2 Bonus Resources" in your workbook.

### The List That Never Ends

Remember, this list is a starting point to help you get inspired to locate information. It is by no means all inclusive. Use it to start your own resource list based on your genre, needs, and format preferences.

I will use these and many other resources in the online course. I will show you how to go from start to finish with a research question. Enroll in the online course if you would like a more thorough understanding of how to apply the knowledge presented in this book, and more.

If you need more inspiration, visit my YouTube channel! I will highlight resources from my own lists and researching sessions. I have interviews with Librarians and authors about their researching tips. I eventually plan to share my visits to world libraries.

**Tip:** Building your own repository of resources is the aim for my work. I will be happy to have you share with me examples of what you have learned from this book. Send me an email at theauthorlibrarian@gmail.com.

**QUESTIONS for 12 Places to Start Your Research Online, Today!**

1. Can you find more sources based on the twelve listed in this chapter?
2. What about the bonuses, are they useful? If so, have you recorded them in your notes?
3. Reflect on each of the sources by analyzing when you may need to access them for your research.
4. Did you wish there was a source listed here you did not see? If so, what was it and why is it important to you in your research? (Send me an email. I will be happy to review it and share it with other authors on the YouTube channel or newer editions of this book.)

# 10

# FINDING YOUR SECRET AGENT

## Experts & How to Interview Them for Research

I WOULD LIKE to dedicate one whole chapter to my favorite type of eyewitness account: the expert interview. I feel like expert interviews are the "secret agents" for clever authors! These types of interviews will help build your understanding of a topic, timeframe, or reinforce a point you wish to make. As a librarian and a research fanatic, I appreciate when an author takes the time to interview experts. In years past, finding experts to interview would have been far more challenging than in the modern digital age.

In this chapter I provide some suggestions to consider when you wish to locate a "secret agent" expert to interview. After that, I will give you tips for interviewing. These tips come from my experience of interviewing over a hundred authors on my podcast.

## Where Can I Find My "Secret Agent?"

It will not take long, after you consider these suggestions, for you to identify where to find an expert to interview.

Some places to consider:

- Podcast interviews.
- Email inquiries you have made to another author.
- Email questions that have come to you based on your work.
- Interviews you have conducted.
- Online interviews you have read.
- Blog posts.
- Speeches from conferences.
- YouTube channels you follow.
- The reference page in the back of a book, encyclopedia, article, or blog.
- Recommendations from other authors.

**ASK A LIBRARIAN:** Honestly, the best way to locate an expert to interview is to ask at your local library. You can discuss your topic with the Librarian. Many Reference Librarians will have leads for you. If they do not, I am positive they would help put the word out on your behalf.

## Don't Be Shy

If you wish to find an expert, don't be nervous. It has been my experience when I have interviewed experts in a field, that they are very willing to talk about their subject. Search across associations and agencies to identify a candidate for your interview.

Spend a little bit of time tracking down an expert based on citations offered in your research.

Do a little bit of cyber investigation. If they are an author in the digital age, you may find them through their own website. Employ a Google search, which is another good way to use Google. Search other platforms that authors may appear on like Goodreads or Amazon. Further, you may be able to find them on Facebook, Instagram, or Twitter.

Look for contact details. If an email is present, use it to reach out.

It is completely okay to reach out with a request to interview. You may even find enough of what they have written, spoken, or shared online that you will not have to have a real interview with them. Just remember, if you use their ideas or actual quotes, to cite them correctly.

Here is one example from my own work that fits this type of expert interview.

Originally, I was setting my historical fiction novels during the Elizabethan era in England. I purchased for my resource library several books on Renaissance England. One author in those books was referred to so often, I had to look him up.

When I did, I was pleasantly surprised to find that he had three non-fiction books that fit my needs. I later discovered he wrote a series of historical fiction on the same time period. I purchased everything I could find by him.

After a little more cyber investigation, I discovered that he had very little media presence. I was unable to track down any contact details.

However, by the time I had read his five books, I had felt that I had already interviewed one of the leading experts of the field. Had I needed more details, I would have asked a Librarian co-worker to help me locate contact information for him.

**Workbook:** Access the "Checklist for Identifying an Expert" in your workbook.

## You Have Identified a "Secret Agent," Now What?

After more than hundred interviews on my podcast, here is practical advice about setting up and conducting an interview:

- Take a few moments to write down the questions you wish to ask. Make sure these questions are open ended to gather the most information.
- Decide the best method for initial contact. Generally, email is considered the most appropriate way for a "cold contact." Cold contact means reaching out to someone who you do not have a relationship with. However, these days, with social media, you can also contact an expert through direct message. I encourage you to use direct messaging to start a conversation to find out if they would be interested in an interview. Then secure an email address to set up the details.
- Set a timeframe from the first contact to reply before your next follow up inquiry. Try to remember that they may be busy. Others may have a team that handles requests. After your reasonable timeframe has passed, send one more request. It is my general rule of thumb that if an expert doesn't get back to me after the second request, I move on. It is also good to decide before the first email how you will conduct the interview:
- Would an email work best?

- Would an interview on Zoom work?
- Most experts will be happy with answering questions via email. This is the format I use the most if I do not wish for them to appear on my podcast or YouTube channel.
- Describe in a succinct email to the expert what information you are seeking, which format you wish to use to gather your information, and any additional requests for your interview.
- When conducting a recorded interview, use a reliable recording method and take notes.
- If conducting an interview via email, check your email for errors, typos, or vague questions.
- Make sure you record the date of the live interview or the date of reply in email for your citations.
- Leave the interview open by asking how they would prefer you to ask follow up questions. Make sure to collect their snail mail address at this time.
- At the end of interview, ask if they can recommend others in their field who would be interested in being included in your work. If so, ask if they are comfortable with you using their name in your first contact email to the individual they recommend.
- Finally, send a thank you note after the interview. If you use their interview in your final work, once the book is published send a signed copy of the book with your acknowledgment of their contribution.

The Best Advice for Interviewing Your "Secret Agent"

Continuously practice your skills of note taking when you are interviewing. Go over your interview notes within 24 hours of the interview. You may find when you take notes, you have an entirely new theme to explore, or you can wrap up an idea that you were wondering about. If you review your notes while the conversation or response is fresh in your head, it will be easier to remember the string of thoughts associated with the interview.

**Workbook:** Access the "Checklist for Conducting an Expert Interview" in your workbook.

## QUESTIONS FOR FINDING **Your Secret Agent**

1. Make a list of where to locate a "secret agent."
2. What holds you back from reaching out to an expert in a field? Do you have a plan to help you get over these struggles? If so, what is that plan?
3. Have you identified a list of expert organizations or associations you wish to explore? Do they have an online presence? If so, what have you learned about their contact information?

# THE AUTHOR'S LIBRARIAN
## IS IN: HOW CAN I HELP?

This May Be The Only Time A Librarian Will Not Ask You To Keep Quiet!

Write A Review!

Share with Your Author Friends!

Thank You -
The Author's Librarian

---

WRITE A REVIEW: Your review will help other writers discover this book!

Let's face it! Despite how knowledgeable you are, how much you have traveled in the world, or how unbiased you believe yourself to be, when you hear the word librarian your mind immediately jumps to a stereotype! Am I wrong? I am guessing not. This is why I am committed to my role as The Author's Librarian. What set into motion my desire to be a librarian led to my discovery of other truths about most librarians. I was hooked.

**Did You enjoy this book?** You can make a big difference.

Reviews are the most powerful tool in my arsenal when it

comes to helping writers find this book. Much as I'd like to, I do not have the financial muscles of a New York publisher.

(Not yet, anyway.)

But what I do have is something far more valuable and something that those publishers would love to get their hands on.

You, my committed and clever readers!

Honest reviews of my book helps bring it to the attention of other readers.

If you enjoyed this book I would be very grateful if you could spend just five minutes leaving a review (it can be as short as you like the book) on my book's Amazon page or Goodreads page. Here are the links to those pages.

Amazon Author page:

**https://www.amazon.com/-/e/B093YGQ8KM**

Goodreads page:

**https://www.goodreads.com/vikjay**

Don't forget to download your copy of the free workbook.

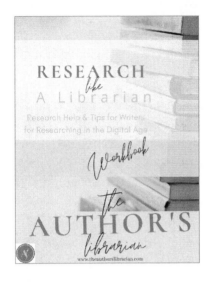

Here is that link again:
https://www.theauthorslibrarian.com/workbook

## My Commitment To You

- Librarians have a deep devotion to community.
- They are guardians of knowledge willing to protect freedom of speech and information.
- Their core belief hinges on access to knowledge for all despite social or economic situations.

I have always been determined to shake up stereotypes. But it wasn't until I became serious about writing novels and the creation of my podcast, "The Authors of the Pacific Northwest," that I understood who I was called to serve.

I am here for you, if you wish to discover how to research

well! I hope you will learn from me within the pages of the books I write, interviews by me in media, through my online courses, from my social media channels, from my websites, and so much more!

You are my why and the reason I am *The Author's Librarian.*

I understand. Writing is hard enough! If I can help one person past the barrier of researching, then all of the dismissive remarks associated with being a Librarian are well worth it.

That being said, I am only one woman! I do have to admit that I have limitations. I wish to share a bit about my teaching style to ensure clarity of what I am able to do as The Author's Librarian.

Over the years of working in higher education, I have discovered that I am an independent learner. Therefore, I work best with students who find ways to become independent learners as well. Independent learners take responsibility for their own learning. They will be self-motivated. Further, they will see frustrations and challenges as a worthwhile step to success. They are often referred to as curious. They will engage in what they learn. Those students that have a goal beyond dependency do extremely well with how I teach!

## Additional Support from The Author's Librarian

**Newsletter:** But that doesn't mean that others cannot learn from me. For those who depend on social learning, I will encourage you to seek out your local librarian for the hands-on practice you need. Sign up for the newsletter here:

https://www.theauthorslibrarian.com/newsletter

**YouTube:** If you wish to dive deeper into the application of researching well, regardless of your learning style, start first with my YouTube channel. The Author's Librarian on YouTube can provide inspiration. It is the only free YouTube channel that

I know of dedicated to authors wishing to get help with researching. Watch the videos here:

https://www.theauthorslibrarian.com/episodes

**Online Courses:** If that is still not enough then enroll in my "Research Like a Librarian" course. In this course we continue the discussion laid out in this book. I will show you how to conduct a research session from start to finish. This course will help you develop the skills needed to be confident in your researching techniques.

I am updating this course to reflect the materials listed in this guide. Here is the waiting list:

https://www.theauthorslibrarian.com/waitlist

Once the course is released: I will notify you.

If you wish to work on your note taking skills, please consider enrolling in my mini course: "Take Notes Like a Librarian." I will help you evaluate several popular note taking tools. I will also show you how you can use these tools to enhance your writing efforts. I am continuing to update this mini course based on the feedback from students. You can sign up for the waiting list here:

https://www.theauthorslibrarian.com/waitlist

I will notify you when that course is released.

**More Guides by The Author's Librarian:** I am also committed to releasing topic related guides soon! Consider joining my mailing list to hear when those will be released.

**How To Reach The Author's Librarian:**

Finally, I realize that I can only scratch the surface on the topic of researching. Considering that limitation, I am committed to answering questions I receive from you. Since most questions will benefit many authors, I will answer many of them directly on my YouTube channel.

Feel free to email me at theauthorlibrarian@gmail.com.

The best way to stay in touch with me regarding the opening

of the online courses, which topics I am covering on the YouTube channel, or when the other guides will be released, is to join my newsletter: From the Stacks | The Author's Librarian Newsletter! Here is the newsletter link:

https://www.theauthorslibrarian.com/newsletter

Cheers to you, clever author!

I hope what you have learned in this book will help you *Research Like A Librarian.*

*Happy Researching!*

AUT*the*HOR'S *librarian*

# DEDICATION

I dedicate this book to my Grandma D. You took me to the public library often, helped me get my first library card, and taught me about the company of books!

# COPYRIGHT

# REFERENCES

## 5. THE "WRITER'S ROOKIE MISTAKE," AKA PLAGIARISM

1. Lipp, C. (2018, December 14). Influence Without Plagiarism: 6 Tips to Avoid an Ailey O'Toole Situation [Article]. Https://Www.Writersdigest.-Com/. https://www.writersdigest.com/write-better-fiction/how-to-draw-influence-from-other-writers-without-plagiarizing-6-tips-to-avoid-an-ailey-otoole-situation
2. Lipp, C.

## 8. HOW TO USE GOOGLE AND WIKIPEDIA LIKE A PRO

1. Turner, E., & Rainie, L. (2020, March 5). Most Americans rely on their own research to make big decisions, and that often means online searches [Web log post]. Retrieved January 19, 2021, from https://www.pewresearch.org/fact-tank/2020/03/05/most-americans-rely-on-their-own-research-to-make-big-decisions-and-that-often-means-online-searches/
2. ZICKUHR, K. (2010, December 10). Generations Online in 2010 [Web log post]. Retrieved January 19, 2021, from https://www.pewresearch.org/internet/2010/12/16/generations-2010/
3. *Oxford Languages and Google - English | Oxford Languages*. (2021, January 10). Oxford Languages and Google - English | Oxford Languages. https://languages.oup.com/google-dictionary-en/
4. "The Office" The Negotiation (TV Episode 2007). (n.d.). IMDb. https://www.imdb.com/title/tt0983623/characters/nm0136797
5. Wikipedia About [Web log post]. (2021, January 22). Retrieved January 23, 2021, from https://en.wikipedia.org/wiki/Wikipedia:About
6. Wikipedia About [Web log post]. (2021, January 22).
7. Wikipedia About [Web log post]. (2021, January 22).
8. Wikipedia About [Web log post]. (2021, January 22).
9. Penn, J. (2018). *How to Write Non-Fiction*. Bath, England: Curl Up Press.

Made in the USA
Monee, IL
19 July 2023

39605749R00083